Bushveld BANQUETS

MYRNA ROBINS

Bushveld BANQUETS

First published in 2006 by Struik Publishers
(a division of New Holland Publishing (South Africa) (Pty) Ltd)
New Holland Publishing is a member of
Johnnic Communications Ltd
Cornelis Struik House, 80 McKenzie Street, Cape Town 8001
86–88 Edgware Road, London, W2 2EA, United Kingdom
14 Aquatic Drive, Frenchs Forest, NSW 2086, Australia
218 Lake Road, Northcote, Auckland, New Zealand

www.struik.co.za

Copyright © in published edition: Struik Publishers 2006
Copyright © in text: Myrna Robins 2006
Copyright © in photographs: Richard van Ryneveld
and Anthony Johnson 2006

page 8 – Jock of the Bushveld – Lanz von Hörsten/IOA
page 9 – Local produce stall – Roger de la Harpe/IOA
pages 27 – Bateleur – Nigel J Dennis/IOA
page 84 – Purple-crested Loerie – Albert Froneman/IOA
page 108 – Rock Monitor – Peter Pickford/IOA
page 109 – Openbilled Stork – Nigel J Dennis/IOA
IOA = Images of Africa

PUBLISHING MANAGER: Linda de Villiers
MANAGING EDITOR: Cecilia Barfield
EDITOR: Irma van Wyk
DESIGNER: Helen Henn
PHOTOGRAPHERS: Richard van Ryneveld
and Anthony Johnson
PROOFREADER: Tessa Kennedy
INDEXER: Joy Clack

Reproduction by COLOR/FUZION
Printed and bound by Sing Cheong Printing Company
Limited, Hong Kong

ISBN 1 77007 288 8 (9 781770 072886)

10 9 8 7 6 5 4 3 2 1

All rights reserved. No part of this publication may be reproduced, stored in a retrieval system or transmitted, in any form or by any means, electronic, mechanical, photocopying, recording or otherwise, without the prior written permission of the publishers and the copyright holders.

Over 40 000 unique African images available to purchase from our image bank at www.imagesofafrica.co.za

AUTHOR'S ACKNOWLEDGEMENTS

Without the support of the lodges and other establishments that feature on these pages, this book would have remained a dream. Thanks to each and every one, and to those who extended us hospitality, our appreciation. Much credit must go to the helpful staff and, of course, to the chefs for their enthusiastic co-operation and delectable creations.

I am indebted to Debby Thomson of Bushveld Connections for supplying me with reams of fascinating information. Special thanks go to Sue Godding, Nicky Williams and John Jackson, all former members of the Bushveld Banquet committee, who have been unfailingly supportive, acting as the northern end of the lifeline on many an occasion.

Acclaimed photographer Anthony Johnson achieved miracles, taking outstanding food pictures at short notice, usually outside and using natural light. The fact that it was the hottest, wettest January in decades merely made him more determined, as he dealt with 40 degree temperatures, howling gales and sheets of rain …

Richard van Ryneveld's beautiful animal pictures, along with those of interiors, exteriors, people and landscapes are testimony to his talent. Here is a person who is always happy to rough it, but who, on this assignment, got more than he was expecting in that line …

To editor Irma van Wyk and designer Helen Henn, both cool, calm and efficient professionals, much appreciation. They were great people with whom to work. To publishing manager Linda de Villiers, whose input has helped Bushveld Banquets to become a reality, my sincere thanks.

As many have said after experiencing life on this extraordinary continent, Africa has its own way of dealing with things, and does so in its own time. That's been borne out during preparation of this title, making it a true child of Africa.

CONTENTS

ABOVE: Becoming environmentally aware is also fun at Southern Cross RIGHT: Headmaster Jumbo Williams with slithery friend

FOREWORD

It is with great pleasure that I draft the foreword for this lovely book. In true fashion, Myrna has left no stone unturned in compiling the well-researched information for this publication. Consequently it is a tribute to her dedication, expertise and hard work, for which she is to be complimented.

Southern Cross is in itself a unique school, its philosophy and ethos making it an apparent global first. It is a school that embraces the natural environment, modern-day educational practices and pupil-centred edification. The school is proudly South African in every sense.

With the school being situated in the heart of the Lowveld and, indeed, the hub of South Africa's eco-tourism industry, the 'Bush Banquet' provides an opportunity to showcase lodge cuisine under one umbrella.

The lodge support of and commitment to the banquet is simply wonderful and indeed greatly appreciated. Their exposure and co-operation is encouraging and further strengthens all that is on offer to the tourists of the region.

The envisioned growth to be developed from this spectacular occasion is the upliftment and training of lodge staff, specifically those involved within the hospitality section.

I proudly endorse this superb publication and hope that many will immerse themselves in the contented preparation and consuming of appetising repasts.

Bon appetit.

Jumbo Williams
HEADMASTER

The Blyde River Canyon, majestic portal to the Lowveld

INTRODUCTION

SETTING THE SCENE

You are about to go on safari through one of South Africa's most enticing and exciting regions. At every scheduled stop, you will not only be accommodated in style, but your taste buds will be tantalised by a feast of Lowveld flavours.

Most of the destinations are situated in low-lying bushveld, in wilderness areas in protected reserves. These are bounded by a line of mountains that not only forms a dramatic backdrop, but also sets the scene for many attractions and activities.

Welcome to the Lowveld, an area that has intrigued adventurers and settlers, pioneers and pilgrims, travellers and fugitives for centuries, with its promise of adventure, wildlife and fertile, well-watered land and seams of gold. It is also a region rich in game, dominated by the expansive Kruger National Park in the east. In addition to this vast national park, the area encompasses some 10 provincial reserves and the world's largest area of privately owned nature reserves.

Many of these, situated along the Kruger Park's western boundary, have dropped their boundary fences, thus vastly increasing the area for wildlife movement. This has, in turn, improved game-viewing opportunities for visitors, making the Lowveld a mecca for viewing the Big Five, where the bush experience can be enjoyed from an open vehicle or on foot.

From many points on this low-lying savanna, less than 600 metres above sea level, an irregular mauve line forms the background: this is the Eastern Escarpment – a natural boundary – which presents a spectacular introduction to the Bushveld, whether arriving by air or by road.

Here the Blyde River Canyon, the third largest canyon in the world, bisects the country from north to south for some 30 km, sheltering indigenous forests along its steep western sides. Both the canyon and its river are major drawcards for visitors, offering not only scenic wonders, but hiking trails and a range of adventure sports.

The Lowveld towns – from Nelspruit in the south, through White River to Sabie and Hazyview, Graskop and Pilgrim's Rest, and on to Hoedspruit and Phalaborwa in the north – each offer their own attractions. Whether they serve as agricultural, mining or forestry centres, they all rely on tourism as an equally important and expanding industry. There are also villages in some rural black areas, such as Bushbuckridge and Acornhoek, that have grown into sizable business centres despite limited infrastructure.

Remembering the Bushveld's most famous canine hero

Hoedspruit was, until quite recently, something of a backwater, barely mentioned in travel guides published in the last quarter of the 20th century. Today this bustling town boasts its own airport and is expanding swiftly, having developed into the hub of Lowveld eco-tourism and a supply centre for game lodges. It is also the site of the Southern Cross Schools and the Bush Banquet, both of which are helping to put Hoedspruit on the educational and gastronomic world map.

The Lowveld falls largely into the province of Mpumalanga, but a broad strip between the Canyon and the Kruger boundary is situated in Limpopo province. The area is known locally as K2C, which stands for Kruger to Canyon.

Kruger to Canyon is also the official name given to the Lowveld Biosphere Reserve that was officially registered by UNESCO in 2002, and launched in Limpopo province in June 2005.

International Biosphere reserves are designated regions where important protected areas lie adjacent to human settlements, which make use of the land in different ways.

The Kruger to Canyon Biosphere encompasses the three elements that guide the biosphere global philosophy: core areas which are securely protected for conservation; clearly identified buffer zones which can be used for co-operative activities like environmental education, recreation and eco-tourism; and a flexible transition area where there are settlements, where agricultural activity takes place and where local communities, non-government organisations and cultural groups can work together.

Along with eco-tourism, there are several development projects on the go in the Lowveld, including

Marketing the Lowveld's colourful produce

local environmental action, a spatial development initiative, academic programmes and groups working to improve the quality of life in rural communities.

Among tourist-related projects are those like the Ivory Route, geared for visitors who want to go beyond wildlife, adventure and beauty, to find out about the earliest inhabitants of the area. They can explore sites where Stone Age relics have been uncovered, see Iron Age settlements and examine artefacts belonging to the Shangaan and Pedi communities.

Even those with no yen for history will stumble into the past in the Lowveld. While many early sites have yet to reveal their secrets, more recent events have been well recorded. Historic highlights are reflected in plaques and signposts, and summarised in brochures waiting to be collected at museums and tourism offices.

It is not difficult to encounter Lowveld settings that evoke the spirit of the past, whether in man-made structures or among rocks on mountain passes. They are likely to be places where hunters and prospectors, soldiers and raiders – and, later, conservationists – have made their mark. Transport riders, pioneer families, even armies tried to tame this country, with limited success. Some stories, not immediately recorded, were altered and embroidered in the retelling, eventually evolving into the stuff of legends, with more than a whiff of mystery to quicken the pulse.

But who needs legends when one can read of the feats of two- and four-legged Lowveld heroes like Harry Wolhuter and Jock of the Bushveld?

Our route to the lodges will take us through a succession of private reserves with evocative names – Kapama, Klaserie, Thornybush, Timbavati, Manyeleti and Sabi Sand. On the way we will pass orchards of subtropical fruit and nuts, a colourful testimony to the importance of farming to the Lowveld economy.

In the south, around Nelspruit, man-made forests are interspersed with groves of pecans and macadamias, which in turn give way to the glossy green of citrus trees and waving banana palms. Around Hazyview rows of avocado trees line the roadside, along with litchi and nut orchards.

Heading north, citrus and mango trees vie for dominance, both bearing a significant percentage of the country's output. Then there are the coffee plantations of the Sabie valley, and the renowned trout streams and farms of the Lydenburg area.

But we are in danger of being sidetracked ... Our safari begins at an extraordinary school on a wildlife estate outside Hoedspruit.

FOLLOWING A STAR

THE RISE OF THE SOUTHERN CROSS SCHOOLS

Imagine a school where girls and boys watch giraffe and warthog, impala and nyala wandering past their playground, on the lookout for a good green meal. And where lessons are learned in a thatched complex on a wildlife estate that looks for all the world like a five-star game lodge.

Lucky learners, amazing surroundings, beautiful buildings – welcome to the Southern Cross Schools.

It seems apposite that the world's first green school, a co-educational establishment with an environmental code as its ethos, be housed in eco-friendly buildings in the centre of South Africa's top eco-tourist region. The Southern Cross Schools outside Hoedspruit is tailormade for its Bushveld setting.

However, like most admirable achievements, it took much inspiration, determination and dogged persistence to make this educational dream a reality.

Its creation and construction were a team effort, but behind the players were two young mothers to whom much of the credit is due.

Shortly before the start of the new millennium, Sue Godding realised that her daughters were no longer toddlers, and that it was time to start thinking about their education. She and her husband Kevin – both working on a game farm in the heart of the Lowveld at the time – are passionate about the Bush and did not relish the idea of leaving in order to give their children a good education.

As other game lodge personnel and managers were in a similar position, it seemed that there was a definite need for an English-medium school in the Hoedspruit district. So Sue called a meeting – a momentous one it proved to be.

About 60 young parents turned up to talk education, and by the end of the evening, a unique concept had evolved – that of a school that would follow the national curriculum while being based on a unique nature-based system.

However, finding funding for and implementing this vision would prove to be a long, hard slog.

Although many parents dropped out, Heidi Smith, who also had two small children at the time, came on board at the start – and stayed. After initial research and consultation with education specialists, the two mothers beavered on as they searched for financial backers for a site, and for an architect and builder sympathetic to their plans, inspiring each other when the going got tough.

Eventually some visionaries came on board, capital was injected, and a deal struck between a developer and the shareholders of a new wildlife estate on the outskirts of Hoedspruit. An architect and builder responsible for five-star game lodges joined the project, and enhanced the land with an attractive thatched complex with walls of ochre and terracotta.

Southern Cross Schools now had a home, and required a sympathetic principal and staff. Jumbo Williams heard about the post while heading an environmental camp in the Kruger Park. A school where an environmental code would serve as a vehicle for instruction fulfilled a long-held dream, and he came aboard with enthusiasm.

In mid-January 2002 the Southern Cross Schools opened to admit the first 40 pupils, which increased to 100 in the second year and 150 at the start of 2004.

At present, the school goes up to grade 9, and there are plans to take pupils through to grade 12 within a year or two.

Boarders are well catered for in Tamboti Lodge, with its secure, home-from-home environment. In this attractive thatched building, up to 40 boys and girls are looked after by house parents. From their windows, children gaze out over the bush to the distant northern Drakensberg. Nearer home, they ride mountain bikes to watch antelope and giraffe at nearby waterholes.

Learning to know and respect nature's creatures

Lowveld teachers meet Southern Cross pupils at weekend workshops

As headmaster Jumbo Williams points out: 'Environmental awareness is no longer a "nice-to-have"; it is mandatory.'

Working on the assumption that environmental awareness is essential for our survival, Southern Cross places high priority on concepts such as sustainable development, environmental integrity and bio-diversity. Programmes have been developed that include hands-on experience to promote the development of life skills, as the school wants its learners to become young adults who are balanced academically, socially, environmentally and culturally, and who are capable of making positive contributions, both to their communities and to the environmental cause.

The Southern Cross, smallest but most distinctive of southern hemisphere constellations, has been an indispensable guide to seafarers and others for many centuries. It makes a fitting name for a school that sets out to guide the next generation wisely and well.

REACH-A-CROSS

Given its philosophy and objectives, it was natural that Southern Cross Schools should instigate an outreach programme regarded as a partnership with rural schools in surrounding areas.

Most of these schools struggle with meagre resources and large numbers. Many of them are also educating a number of Aids orphans, children from as young as 10 who head households with younger siblings, and lack any secure source of income.

The Reach-A-Cross project members formulated several objectives after meeting with various stakeholders in local communities. It was decided that educational strategies needed to be designed and implemented to help local teachers.

The programme would also be used to bring together future generations and to promote a culture of service beyond self.

After interaction with circuit managers and other Education Department officials, Reach-A-Cross planned workshops and forums at a number of venues, where teachers and project officials meet to develop ways of making the best use of resources. These have proved very successful, with teachers and staff often travelling many kilometres to the venues.

The first workshop of 2006 was held at the Southern Cross Schools, where the theme of Lesson Planning and Assessment was addressed. As always, the positive

Teaching the teachers at a Reach-A-Cross workshop

reaction from those attending was overwhelming and offered a humbling experience for the Southern Cross staff who took part.

Teachers at hundreds of schools across Limpopo and Mpumalanga have already benefited from these workshops, and this, in turn, has positively affected many thousands of learners.

Reach-A-Cross also operates a bursary trust that enables children from underprivileged communities to attend lessons at Southern Cross, while their Educator Cadetship programme identifies community learners who wish to train as teachers, bringing them in to Southern Cross for their tertiary education.

Similarly, learners who want to become trackers – a qualification much in demand by the eco-tourism industry – also receive aid in achieving their goals.

In addition, children from needy schools join fellow learners from Southern Cross on school trips to the Kruger National Park as part of the environmental awareness programmes.

There is also an exchange programme and project started by the Southern Cross learners themselves called Kids4Kids. It includes fund-raising, visiting physically disadvantaged children, and helping schools to improve resources.

This year a neglected primary school, approximately 15 kilometres from Hoedspruit, is the beneficiary, acquiring a facelift, furniture and equipment. And so the dream continues to flourish and expand, and to reach across and make a significant contribution to community and country. Although stakeholders and corporate donors help fund operational costs, the quest for financial support is ongoing. Your purchase of this book has helped this worthy cause, one that is part of and true to the African dream, and it is greatly appreciated.

CHALLENGING THE CHEFS

While some tented kitchens are sophisticated and stylishly decorated, others are simply trestle tables under a canvas sheet. But they all shelter chefs and assistants who are whipping up epicurean fare in pretty primitive conditions. As the shadows lengthen, fires flicker and gas lamps hiss while cooks peel and dice, steam and stir-fry. Soon an array of mouth-watering aromas joins the wood smoke drifting on the breeze. Nerves become taut, and the tension is palpable as the hour of reckoning draws near at the Bush Banquet Challenge …

Well-appointed table at the 2002 Banquet

THE BIRTH OF THE BUSH BANQUET

The Bush Banquet marked its fifth anniversary in 2006. From comparatively humble beginnings this gastronomic contest has developed into a delicious, prominent, nail-biting annual event where artistically plated fare is presented to judges and guests in a spirit of keen but friendly rivalry.

It takes place in the grounds of the Southern Cross Schools, and involves the chefs and kitchen teams of a wide array of top lodges, smaller bush camps, culinary schools and country hotels from across the Lowveld and beyond. It is a great opportunity for talented chefs to demonstrate innovation, ingenuity and gastronomic expertise, as they have to create and serve three-course gourmet dinners for 10 in tented kitchens in the school grounds a few hours ahead of the banquet.

Fund-raising has always been an essential element of the founding and running of the Southern Cross Schools. Soon after it opened in 2002, Sue Godding and Heidi Smith needed to raise money for a prize-giving function, and this is when the idea of a bush banquet was mooted. The first one took place soon afterwards, bringing together Lowveld chefs and lodge personnel, residents and parents, farmers and townsfolk.

The initial event was so popular and successful that the number of contestants doubled in 2003. With each successive year the competition has gained both in prestige and prominence, now taking its place as one of South Africa's top culinary events. It usually takes place in May, when the evenings are cool and dry.

On the day of the Banquet the school grounds are a hive of activity as team members start dressing their tables in the courtyard while the chefs set up their camp kitchens.

This table saluted the Sotho culinary heritage

The cooks are limited to using wood and gas as fuel, are supplied with water and ice, and can pre-prepare their first courses and desserts. But main courses have to be produced from scratch.

Guests start arriving well before dark. Having paid handsomely for their seats, they are ready to dine well, be entertained and enjoy the party. Judges, meanwhile, circulate to appraise the table settings before settling to taste-test each course from every entrant.

As a former judge I can attest to the difficulty in finding a winner from among the beautifully dressed tables: a rich Moroccan set-up seduces with huge cushions and napery in scarlet and gold, contrasting with the crisp snowy linen of a contemporary setting across the way. An Out-of-Africa theme makes a statement in khaki and cream in one corner, while a simple design featuring silver and fresh greenery offers fresh appeal in another.

As moonlight adds its glow to the scene, aromas mingle as savoury delights are served to hungry diners. Then it's time to be entertained by celebrities from all over South Africa, before an auction of artwork takes place. When the time arrives for the results to be announced, loud cheers ring out from tables belonging to the winning lodges. As there are several categories and two divisions, the prize-giving takes a while to complete. Coffee is served, the music starts and the party is on …

The Bush Banquet Challenge brings in a sizable sum for Southern Cross Schools and the Reach-A-Cross programmes. While the Challenge is an annual event, Lowveld chefs are expected to produce delectable fare three times a day, seven days a week for guests who are paying handsomely for their Bushveld holiday.

Although better roads, refrigerated trucks and locally grown seasonal produce combine to make their lives much easier than those of the early bush cooks, today higher standards are expected, and chefs need to keep in touch with global culinary trends wherever they find themselves.

Diners usually enjoy a variety of venues during their stay, with meals being presented in bomas, dining areas, riverbeds and under the stars, with the distant roar of predators hunting for their supper as background music.

The daily ritual of early morning game drives and bush walks makes for dining patterns that start with tea, coffee and rusks or muffins around 6 am, followed by a hearty brunch after the drive. Lunch is often a light affair, with high tea setting the scene for the evening drive, and dinner being served after 8 pm.

Occasionally disaster strikes, and with no corner café to run to, this is where the ingenuity of Bushveld chefs comes into play. They can produce delicious fare relying on their stock cupboards, using bottles and cans with dexterity and raiding the garden for whatever the porcupines have left …

Game lodge chefs have been criticised by city foodies for neglecting to include game meat on their menus. While a few include the occasional venison dish, most stay with conventional red meat as the majority of diners are squeamish about finding game meat (or even game bird) on their plate, having admired the living version in the bush an hour before.

But whether it's stylish and formal or a rustic barbecue, Bushveld banquets are often memorable meals, accompanied by good Cape wine and wide and friendly smiles. It's time to set off on our gastronomic quest for bountiful breakfasts, languid lunches, zesty game drive snacks and scrumptious suppers that finish with dreamy desserts.

TINTSWALO

TINTSWALO SAFARI LODGE

Our first visit to Tintswalo took place soon after flying into the Lowveld. We were tired and stressed from city life and work. Passing through the heavy doors of the manor house, with its dry-stone walls and conical roof of thatch, was akin to entering the portals of another world. The sensation was reinforced as we savoured high tea on a deck shaded by the boughs of a 500-year-old Jackalberry, watching buffalo and baboon in the riverbed below. Taut shoulders and fatigue gave way to newfound energy and heightened anticipation – the Lowveld was working its magic both speedily and efficiently …

Enter Tintswalo and discover Lowveld luxury

Manyeleti, the Shangaan word for Place of the Stars, is a game reserve that shares its eastern boundary with the Kruger National Park and borders the Sabi Sand Game Reserve in the south. This is where Tintswalo is located, a fairly new lodge that has not taken long to garner its fair share of accolades, both locally and internationally.

Stone walls and raggedy-edge thatch enclose the spacious, inviting suites, each featuring full-length glass doors that open onto private decks with plunge pools.

The suites are individually decorated, each inspired by the story of a British or European explorer famous for 19th century expeditions undertaken to 'discover' the dark continent. The luxurious colonial décor, with extra-long double beds, indoor and outdoor showers, air-conditioning and mini-bars, adds up to accommodation of a standard beyond the wildest dreams of Livingstone and Stanley, Burton and Speke.

Guests can also book an ultra-luxurious suite or the Presidential suite, the latter being the only place where children are accommodated.

The Elan Vital spa at Tintswalo entices guests to take advantage of a range of facial and body treatments for both sexes.

Tastebuds are constantly tantalised as the cuisine is of an enviably high standard – a fact reflected in the two Bush Banquet Challenges that Tintswalo has entered. After being placed in several categories in 2004, they repeated this feat in 2005, capping it by coming second overall in the Gold Category.

Innovative quality characterises chef Develing's creations

Executive chef Jenna Develing and her team present innovative contemporary fare, which includes some imaginative breakfast dishes.

Given these gastronomic temptations, it's as well that Tintswalo schedules a variety of walks to counter the kilojoules: guests can go birding and stargazing, while adventurous souls can also book sleep-outs in the bush.

Education Alive Limpopo is an ongoing community project started in 1998 to improve the standard of education. Many teachers and students have benefited from study courses, reflected in vastly improved results in the pass rate at local schools. A percentage of Tintswalo's turnover is donated to this fund.

CARAMELISED PINEAPPLE PASTRY WITH YOGHURT AND HONEY

Breakfast choices do not come better than this delicious creation from Tintswalo's kitchen.

200 g butter, preferably unsalted, softened
60 ml (4 T) brown sugar
30 ml (2 T) icing sugar
2 queen pineapples, peeled, cored and sliced thickly into rounds
1 sheet puff pastry, defrosted if frozen
100 ml honey
5 ml (1 t) Chinese five-spice powder
natural yoghurt
berries to garnish
mint sprigs to garnish

Preheat the oven to 200 °C. Mix the butter with both sugars, spread it out on a baking tray, and arrange the pineapple rings on the mixture, turning to coat. Place in the oven and let the mixture caramelise for about 15 minutes, taking care not to brown it too much. Reduce the heat to 180 °C. Cut 8 cm diameter circles from the pastry and arrange on a greased baking tray. Grease a second tray and place it, greased side down, over the pastry circles. Bake for 10 minutes, then increase the heat to 200 °C and bake for a further 10 minutes, or until golden. Remove the top tray and let the pastry cool. Meanwhile, combine the honey and spice powder, bring to the boil, remove from the heat, and leave to infuse.

To serve, anchor a pastry circle in the centre of a plate with a drop of spiced honey. Top with a pineapple ring, then add a dollop of yoghurt to the centre of the ring. Repeat the layer with pastry, pineapple and yoghurt. Drizzle honey over the pineapple and around the plate. Garnish with berries and mint.

Serves 4–5

PUMPKIN SEED AND CHILLI FRITTERS

These zesty bites are offered to guests with drinks at sunset during game drives. A simple dipping sauce of natural yoghurt spiced with dried coriander will team well.

oil for deep-frying
500 ml (2 cups) flour
10 ml (2 t) baking powder
150 g pumpkin seeds, toasted and chopped
2 fresh red chillies, seeded and finely chopped
1 fresh green chilli, seeded and finely chopped
15 ml (1 T) freshly chopped coriander leaves
5 ml (1 t) freshly grated root ginger
15 ml (1 T) sweet chilli sauce
250 ml (1 cup) water
1 extra-large egg
salt and pepper
1 egg white

In a deep-fryer preheat the oil to about 180 °C . Also preheat the oven to 180 °C. Sieve the flour and baking powder together. Add the chopped seeds, chillies, coriander and ginger to the flour mixture. Combine the chilli sauce, water and egg in a small bowl. Make a well in the flour and stir in the egg mixture. Season the batter. Whisk the egg white until soft peaks form, then fold into the batter. Fry tablespoons of batter in batches of no more than 5 at a time for about 5 minutes. Drain on paper towel, then place on baking trays and bake for about 10 minutes. Serve warm or at room temperature, adding a dipping sauce, if wanted.

Makes ±20 small fritters

ICED TIRAMISU

If you cannot find amaretti biscuits, use ginger nuts, recommends Chef Develing.

500 ml (2 cups) mascarpone cheese
50 ml (3 rounded T) cream
3 eggs
200 g castor sugar
200 ml (⅘ cup) Amaretto™ liqueur
100 ml espresso coffee
750 g amaretti biscuits
cocoa powder
berries or fruit to accompany (optional)

Mix the mascarpone and cream together until smooth. Whisk the eggs until foamy. Heat the castor sugar slowly until it just starts to colour at the sides, then slowly pour the hot sugar onto the whisked eggs, whisking continuously until all is used and the mixture becomes thick and glossy. Continue whisking until it cools. When quite cold, mix in the mascarpone mixture. Heat the Amaretto™ and espresso together, stirring. Line a baking tin (at least 5 cm deep) with greaseproof paper and arrange half the biscuits over the base. Pour over half of the liqueur and coffee mixture. Spoon half of the mascarpone mixture evenly over the soaked biscuits. Dip the remaining biscuits in the remaining liqueur and coffee mixture, and arrange over the mascarpone. Top with the remaining mascarpone, smoothing the top. Freeze for at least 2 hours until set. To serve, cut into triangles, squares or circles and sprinkle over a little cocoa powder. Garnish with berries or sliced seasonal fruit.

Serves 8–10

AKERU SAFARI LODGE

A bateleur eagle regularly circles the skies above Akeru and, very occasionally, alights. This magnificent raptor keeps watch over a delightful lodge where guests reconnect with nature and where children of all ages are welcome. When we arrived, a couple of warthog was standing disconsolately near a spread of vygies. Having demolished the lawn, they didn't find the replacement vegetation to their taste. As Tammy McLintock took us from the pool area into the comfy lounge and adjoining dining room, visitors paused to greet us. Enveloped by this homely atmosphere, we saw it would be easy to arrive as guests and leave as friends.

A bateleur eagle watches over Akeru

Intrepid Lowvelder Tammy McLintock

Akeru has been described as a refuge in the Timbavati wilderness, a place where you can find your inner self while absorbing a real bush experience.

The lodge can only accommodate 16 guests, making it an attractive destination for gatherings of friends and families. A significant percentage of visitors, both South African and international, return at least once, some more than once.

While reception rooms and bedrooms offer every creature comfort, McLintock's eco-friendly, back-to-nature philosophy dictates that electricity be eschewed in favour of lanterns. The en-suite chalets, which are individually decorated, have battery-powered fans, and gas geysers heat the water.

The rangers who lead guests on bush walks or game drives concentrate as much on the smaller creatures as they do on the Big Five.

Serene and inviting as Akeru is, it's a success story that is tinged with sadness. The site was a dream venture of young Wayne McLintock, a ranger with a deep passion for the bush, dedicated to conservation and preservation. As he and his wife Tammy started the huge task of transforming the neglected camp that was there into one for special wilderness retreats, Wayne was diagnosed with leukaemia.

He died in 2003. Tammy continued alone, developing the little lodge in the way that they had planned. Today she is still passionate about every aspect of Akeru, exhibiting boundless energy both on site and on marketing forays.

The staff at Akeru seem to have absorbed positive energy from their surroundings, projecting an image of enjoying what they do. A cheerful team of female chefs present well-cooked meals, including colourful lunch buffets of hot dishes, crisp salads and delicious home-baked breads.

Shortly after Wayne McLintock's death, the bateleur eagle started putting in regular appearances above Akeru. On the day this large black and white bird first alighted on a rock in the camp, Tammy's small daughter Therese remarked matter-of-factly to her mother: 'There's daddy.' Since then Tammy has felt certain that – far from being a figment of her imagination – the protective spirit present at Akeru prefers to materialise as a magnificent winged raptor.

AKERU'S EARLY MORNING HEALTH RUSKS

Home-baked rusks and coffee make a favourite start to the South African day, especially if there's an early-morning game drive on the menu.

1 kg self-raising flour
10 ml (2 t) salt
10 ml (2 t) baking powder
500 ml (2 cups) brown sugar
500 ml (2 cups) rolled oats
750 ml (3 cups) All-Bran Flakes®
500 ml (2 cups) sunflower seeds
250 g seedless raisins (optional)
2 eggs
500 ml (2 cups) buttermilk
500 g butter, melted

Combine the dry ingredients. Whisk together the eggs, buttermilk and melted butter. Combine the two mixtures and mix to a dough. Spoon into a large, deep, greased baking tin and smooth the top. Using a sharp knife, mark out rectangles, which will make it easier to break into rusks after drying.

Bake at 180 °C for 30 minutes to 1 hour, depending on the oven and thickness of the rusks. Remove from the oven, leave to cool slightly, then turn out onto a wire rack and cool completely. Break into fingers, return to a baking tin and dry the rusks out in a cool oven for about 4 hours or leave them in the warming drawer overnight. Depending on the size, this recipe will yield 80–100 rusks.

AKERU'S PANCAKES FILLED WITH SMOKED CHICKEN AND MANGO

These trendy wraps are typical of the appetising, crunchy, wholesome fare guests relish for lunch at Akeru.

PANCAKES
250 ml (1 cup) flour
pinch of salt
1 egg, beaten
15 ml (1 T) oil
250 ml (1 cup) milk
additional oil for frying

FILLING
oil
6 baby corncobs (mealies), cut into strips
3 carrots, pared and cut into strips
4 baby marrows (courgettes), trimmed and cut into strips
½ bunch spring onions, chopped
1 red pepper, cored, seeded and cut into strips
1 yellow pepper, cored, seeded and cut into strips
bean sprouts (optional)
2 smoked chicken fillets, shredded
1 fresh mango, peeled and diced or 1–2 canned mangoes, drained and chopped
salt and pepper to taste
1 small bunch fresh coriander leaves, coarsely chopped

For the pancakes, sieve the flour and salt into a bowl. Make a well in the centre and add the egg, oil and a little milk. Using a wooden spoon, mix well, then beat in the remaining milk, a little at a time. The batter must be smooth and have the consistency of thin cream. Leave it to rest for an hour or two.

To cook, heat a little oil in a pan, pour in enough batter to cover the base, and cook on each side until pale brown. Stack the pancakes, separated with plastic wrap, and keep warm. Makes 8–10 pancakes.

For the filling, heat a little oil in a wok or large frying pan, add the first 6 ingredients and the sprouts, if using, and stir-fry over fairly high heat until the vegetables start to wilt, but retain their crunch. Remove from the heat. Add the shredded chicken and mango, and season to taste.

Stir in the fresh coriander, then divide the filling between the pancakes.

Roll up, garnish with herbs and serve with a side salad.

Wine pairing: Enhance this colourful lunch dish with a glass of chilled KWV Laborie Chardonnay.

Serves 8

LABORIE
CHARDONNAY

AKERU'S BREAD AND BUTTER PUDDING WITH BANANAS AND AMARULA CREAM™ SAUCE

Amarula™ is a popular South African liqueur made from the fruit of the Marula tree, which is indigenous to the Lowveld.

6–8 slices white bread or currant loaf
butter
2–3 bananas, sliced
2 eggs
60 ml (4 T) sugar
750 ml (3 cups) milk
5 ml (1 t) vanilla essence

AMARULA CREAM™ SAUCE
250 ml (1 cup) sugar
125 ml (115 g) butter
15 ml (1 T) water
250 ml (1 cup) cream or full-cream milk
±45 ml (3 T) Amarula™

Butter the bread generously and arrange, buttered side down, in a baking dish.
Tuck the banana slices between the bread.
Beat together the eggs, sugar, milk and vanilla essence. Pour this mixture over the bread and leave to soak for 30 minutes.
Cover the dish with foil, and bake in a preheated oven at 160–180 °C for 30 minutes.
Remove the foil and continue baking until the top is nicely browned.
For the sauce, combine the sugar, butter and water in a small pan, stirring until the mixture starts to caramelise and change colour. Watch closely at this stage, as it burns easily.
Remove from the heat and stir in the cream or milk and the liqueur.
Reheat, stirring until the sauce is smooth, then pour carefully over the hot pudding.
Serves 6–8

Motswari Game Reserve

Wandering between the thatched rondavels – dotted around a sweep of lawn and shaded by venerable trees – I was transported back to childhood holidays at resorts that share similarities with Motswari. There is a timelessness here, even a touch of nostalgia, so it came as little surprise to learn that this is the oldest lodge in the Timbavati Game Reserve, one which has been offering visitors tranquil seclusion and exciting game viewing for 30 years. Its position deep in the Bushveld, isolated from roads and the noise of passing vehicles, makes this family-owned private reserve a true getaway destination.

Elephant evidence at Motswari

Long-standing employee and head chef Grace Mnisi

When two Johannesburg businessmen invested in this reserve deep in the Timbavati, they were among the pioneers of the lodge industry. Today, although Motswari offers all the contemporary facilities the modern traveller expects, the camp has managed to retain an appealing old-fashioned ambience.

Understated luxury is one of the keynotes at Motswari, emphasised by décor that favours natural hues and textures. Guests stay in one of 15 air-conditioned rondavels, each distinguished by its earthy hue and animal name. Furnishings are lent a colonial feel with kists, Nguni skin rugs and white drapery. Bathrooms are modern, and each rondavel opens onto a private stoep.

One gravitates effortlessly to the welcoming reception area where heavy beams support a substantial thatched roof, housing a long bar and overlooking the swimming pool and usually dry Sohebele riverbed.

When stepping into the more formal lounge, modern communication facilities contrast with a gallery of family photographs that span more than three decades and some interesting works of art, produced by a talented family member.

Game drives to see the Big Five and more may be augmented by safari walks, and the camp accommodates small conference groups.

Motswari's general manager Kathy Bergs welcomes guests with natural charm and a distinct American accent. The story of how this former New York bank manager visited this bush camp on holiday some 20 years ago – and stayed – is worth hearing. Several former colleagues, who were horrified to hear that she was exchanging corporate life for one in the bush, are enthusiastic visitors to Motswari today.

Kathy and Steve Bergs preside over a team of hospitable staff that includes another long-standing member of staff. Head chef Grace Mnisi, whose grandfather presided in the kitchen in the mid-1970s, worked her way from scullery maid to her present position, and presents a succession of delectable meals to appreciative guests.

Motswari has been a contestant in the Bush Banquet for three consecutive years and in 2005 it was placed among the top entrants in the categories of Best Kitchen and Food and Wine pairing.

POLENTA CORN CAKES WITH AVOCADO AND PEPPADEW™ SALSA

Stylish African starter that will appeal as much to carnivores as to vegetarians.

POLENTA CORN CAKES
500 ml (2 cups) polenta
60 ml (4 T) grated Parmesan cheese
60 g butter, softened
2 eggs, lightly beaten
1 x 410 g can whole kernel corn, drained
500 ml (2 cups) milk
5 ml (1 tsp) salt
pinch pepper
375 ml (1½ cups) self-raising flour
oil for frying

AVOCADO PURÉE
flesh of 3 ripe avocados, mashed
5 ml lemon juice or to taste
salt and pepper

PEPPADEW™ SALSA
165 g peppadews™, chopped
1 small onion, chopped
1 small sweet red pepper, seeded, cored and chopped
20 ml (4 t) olive oil
60 ml (4 T) red wine vinegar
salt and ground black pepper
rocket leaves

Make the corn cakes by combining all the ingredients and mixing well. Form into cakes using 2 tablespoons. Heat a little oil and fry the cakes on both sides until golden brown and cooked through. Drain on paper towel and keep warm. For the purée, combine the avocado and lemon juice and season. For the salsa, combine all the ingredients, except the rocket, and season to taste. Serve by placing the rocket on a plate to form a star. Top with one or two corn cakes and finish with a spoonful of avocado purée and another of salsa.
Serves up to 10

OSTRICH FILLET WITH A PEPPERCORN CRUST AND RED WINE JUS

Ostrich makes an excellent substitute for red meat, being lean and flavourful, but has a tendency to dry out, so do not overcook.

1 large ostrich fillet
30 ml (2 T) oil
15 ml (1 T) ground coriander
30 ml (2 T) paprika
5 ml (1 t) cumin seeds
10 ml (2 t) curry powder
10 ml (2 t) black pepper
30 ml (2 T) dried mixed herbs

PEPPERCORN AND GREEN PESTO CRUST
80 ml (⅓ cup) whole coriander, crushed
125 ml (½ cup) whole black peppercorns, crushed
60 ml (4 T) chopped parsley
125 ml (½ cup) sweet chilli sauce
250 ml (1 cup) pesto (basil paste)

RED WINE JUS
80 ml (⅓ cup) cornflour
500 ml (2 cups) dry red wine
750 ml (3 cups) beef stock
30 ml (2 T) Worcestershire sauce

Rub the fillet on all sides with the oil, then rub in the spices and herbs, cover with plastic wrap and leave for about 30 minutes.

Grill the meat under a preheated grill until medium rare or to taste. Combine the ingredients for the peppercorn and pesto crust and spread over the top of the meat, then return it to the grill until a crust has formed. Keep the fillet warm. Combine the ingredients for the jus in a saucepan, bring to a simmer, stirring, and cook until thickened. Serve slices of fillet with the jus and baby vegetables of choice. Wine pairing suggestion: Ostrich and Merlot make excellent companions, so KWV Cathedral Cellar Merlot is a good bet, but the robust flavours should also be well complemented by the KWV Reserve Cabernet Sauvignon.

Serves 6

GRACE'S GINGER PUDDING WITH PEARS, CINNAMON ICE CREAM AND BUTTERSCOTCH SAUCE

Lowveld winter nights can be surprisingly chilly, which is when a comforting dessert like this comes into its own.

90 g butter
80 ml (⅓ cup) brown sugar
2 eggs
60 ml (4 T) cake flour
160 ml (⅔ cup) self-raising flour
5 ml (1 t) ground cinnamon
5 ml (1 t) ground ginger
30 ml (2 T) milk

TOPPING
80 ml (⅓ cup) brown sugar
7 ml (1½ t) water
10 ml (2 t) butter
30 ml (2 T) chopped glacé ginger

POACHED PEARS
250 ml (1 cup) castor sugar
500 ml (2 cups) water
1 cinnamon stick
3 firm pears, peeled, cored and halved lengthwise

cinnamon ice cream, preferably home-made

BUTTERSCOTCH SAUCE
50 g butter
125 ml (½ cup) brown sugar, firmly packed
300 ml thickened cream

Cream the butter and sugar until light and fluffy. Add the eggs, one at a time, beating well after each addition. Sift the flours and spices together. Combine half of the flour mixture and half of the milk with the egg mixture, and stir. Repeat with the remaining flour and milk.

Grease 6 x half-cup capacity ovenproof moulds and line the bases with greaseproof paper. To make the topping, combine the sugar, water and butter in a small pan, stirring until the sugar has dissolved. Boil for 1 minute, then stir in the ginger. Divide the pudding batter evenly between the moulds, then pour over the topping mixture. Cover the moulds with greased foil, place in a *bain-marie* and bake at 180 °C for about 25 minutes or until cooked through. Leave for 5 minutes before turning out onto serving plates.

Make a syrup of the castor sugar, water and cinnamon stick, add the pear halves, cover with greaseproof paper, then simmer until just tender. Leave to cool in the syrup.

For the butterscotch sauce, combine the butter and sugar in a pan, heat and stir until the sugar has dissolved. Stir in the cream, and simmer for about 5 minutes or until the sauce is slightly thickened.

Serve the puddings accompanied by half a poached pear and scoops of cinnamon ice cream, drizzled with warm butterscotch sauce.

Serves 6

ROYAL MALEWANE

It seems that even the Big Five extend royal treatment to visitors here. Our ranger took his seat behind the wheel and jokingly took orders ahead of our last game drive … The Japanese wanted lion, the British requested elephant and an American asked for rhino. Not ten minutes later, three female lions and assorted teenagers and cubs yawned and waved paws as they rolled on their backs alongside the track. The rhino were too busy grazing and left it to the elephant to perform. Two three-month-old jumbos stepped forward from protective adults to demonstrate their soccer skills, kicking a large stone back and forth with enthusiasm.

Elephant are seldom far from Royal Malewane

Royal Malewane is about 50 km from Hoedspruit, lying within the greater Kruger National Park in a 12 000 ha reserve where excellent game viewing is virtually guaranteed. Few leave without seeing the Big Five and much more during morning and evening drives led by experienced rangers and a master tracker – one of only two in South Africa.

This splendid and opulent destination hosts a maximum of 20 guests, offering privacy, personal service, and the largest suites in Africa. Those who choose Royal Malewane enjoy not only spacious, elegantly furnished hideaways, but can call on the services of a private butler, chef, masseuse and ranger.

But right royal treatment is meted out to all visitors: from the minute they reach the awe-inspiring entrance, guarded by two bronze cheetahs, they are enveloped in a Bushveld paradise, where the reception area leads to an open-air dining room, lounge and library, furnished with antiques and Persian carpets.

The six freestanding suites entice relaxation, whether on daybeds under gazebos on the private deck, bush-gazing from the plunge pool, or sipping sherry in front of the colonial-style fireplace in the living room. Canopied beds and beautifully appointed bathrooms complete these tranquil oases.

Royal Malewane recently extended and refurbished their spa, offering health and skin-care therapies administered by internationally qualified therapists in idyllic surroundings.

General Manager John Jackson, celebrated chef and passionate gardener

The lodge is renowned for its gourmet cuisine, created by a talented team under the watchful eye of General Manager John Jackson, a celebrated chef whose reputation for delectable haute cuisine extends far beyond the African continent.

Along with an impressive list of international awards, Royal Malewane has hosted many local and international celebrities over the years, many of whom return whenever they can escape hectic schedules.

Some go on to enjoy Malewane's equally splendid sister resorts in the Western Cape at Franschhoek and Hermanus, for a triple treat incorporating bush, burg and bay in a memorable package.

Royal Malewane has taken part in the Bush Banquet since inception, winning awards for table, food and service, and, in 2005, the prize for Best Food and Wine pairing.

CORONATION PRAWN AND SALMON SALAD WITH POPPADUMS, PINEAPPLE AND AVOCADO

In keeping with its surroundings, this is an impressive first course that looks and tastes luxurious, yet is not difficult to make, although it requires a little dexterity to plate.

8 queen prawns
200 g fresh, filleted salmon
olive oil
salt and pepper
8 peeled slices of ripe queen pineapple
500 ml (2 cups) vanilla syrup
vegetable oil for deep-frying
4 poppadums (available from Indian shops)
assorted salad leaves
1 ripe avocado

CORONATION SAUCE
250 ml (1 cup) mayonnaise
30 g fruit chutney
30 g sweet chilli sauce
5–10 ml (1–2 t) medium-strength curry powder
salt and white pepper

Shell the prawns, remove the heads and devein. Poach in salted boiling water until just cooked, refresh in cold water, then chill. Cut the salmon into 4 wedges, brush with olive oil, season and chill. Cook the pineapple slices in the vanilla syrup until tender. Cool, then chill.

For the Coronation sauce combine all the ingredients and season to taste. Toss the prawns gently in the sauce. Just before serving, transfer the salmon to a preheated oven at 210 °C and roast until just cooked.

Heat the oil and deep-fry the poppadums one at a time until puffed and crispy. Drain on paper towel.

To serve, divide the salad leaves between 4 plates. Top with overlapping pineapple slices. Fan the peeled avocado and place slices opposite the pineapple. Add the salmon and cold prawns, topping with the remaining sauce. Prop up a poppadum behind the seafood.

Serves 4

LIGHTLY CURRIED VICHYSSOISE TOPPED WITH LEEK AND POTATO STIR-FRY

A warm and lightly spiced version of a Gallic classic.

50 ml (3 T plus 1 t) olive oil
15 ml (1 T) mild curry powder, or to taste
4 large potatoes, peeled, 3½ cubed
2 leeks, washed, and 1½ sliced
4 cloves garlic, 3 finely chopped
2 vegetable stock cubes
500 ml (2 cups) hot water
250 ml (1 cup) milk
250 ml (1 cup) cream
cornflour (optional)
salt and pepper
30 g butter
4 chives, finely snipped

Heat the oil, add the curry powder, cubed potato, sliced leeks and chopped garlic, and sauté until the vegetables start to colour. Add the stock cubes dissolved in the hot water, bring to a simmer and cook until the vegetables are very tender. Remove from the heat, add the milk and blend the soup until smooth. Stir in the cream and check the consistency – if too thin, thicken with a little cornflour made into a paste with water. Season to taste and reheat.

Dice the remaining potato, finely slice the remaining leek and finely chop the remaining garlic. Heat the butter and sauté the vegetables until they start to crisp and brown. To serve, ladle hot soup into 4 bowls, top with the stir-fried vegetables and sprinkle with chives.

Serves 4

GRILLED SALMON WITH GALETTE OF POTATO AND FINE BEANS

A simple but delicious combination of textures and flavours star in this French-style creation.

800 g fresh salmon fillet
olive oil
salt
black pepper
1 large punnet fine green beans
250 g Gorgonzola cheese
4 large potatoes
vegetable oil
250 ml (1 cup) pouring cream
cornflour

Cut the salmon into 4 equal portions. Place on a greased baking sheet, brush with olive oil, grind on salt and black pepper and chill until required.

Top and tail the beans and blanch, uncovered, in boiling water until just tender. Refresh in iced water, drain and cover with wet paper towel.

Cut half of the cheese into 1 cm cubes, and the remainder into 2 cm cubes.

Shortly before serving, wash and peel the potatoes, but do NOT wash again after peeling. Dribble just enough olive and vegetable oil, half of each, into a dinner plate-size frying pan to form a fine film on the base. Slice the potatoes thinly and arrange on the oil, overlapping the slices to resemble the petals of a flower. Heat the pan, and fry the potato galette until the underside is crisp and brown, turn it over and fry the other side. Place on paper towel on a baking sheet and make three more galettes.

Preheat the oven grill until very hot, then grill the salmon until slightly under-cooked. Remove the galettes from the paper towel, reheat in the warm oven and reheat the beans in the cream. Thicken the cream with a paste made from a little cornflour and water, then fold in all the Gorgonzola cubes.

To serve place a galette on each of four heated plates, top with the salmon, pile the beans halfway over the salmon, and dribble a little cream sauce from the beans over both fish and beans.

Serves 4

GRILLED DUCK BREAST WITH CAPE RATATOUILLE SERVED WITH A CAPE PORT SAUCE

When guests are seated at tables glittering with silver and crystal and are served sophisticated fare like this, it's easy to forget where they are – until the distant roar of lions and bark of baboons remind them of their bush setting.

CAPE RATATOUILLE
50 ml (3 T plus 1 t) olive oil
125 ml (½ cup) of each of the following, diced: butternut (or pumpkin), sweet potato, carrot, aubergine, onion, red and yellow pepper, and baby marrow
250 ml (1 cup) very ripe, diced tomato
50 ml (3 T plus 1 t) tomato purée
pinch each of very finely chopped lavender, thyme, Italian parsley, sage, basil and rosemary
5 ml (1 t) finely diced garlic
salt and ground black pepper

PORT SAUCE
300 ml good meat stock
150 ml Cape port
20 g cold butter

2 large potatoes, cooked in their jackets
vegetable oil for deep-frying

2 large duck breasts
olive oil

Make the ratatouille: Heat the oil in a large deep pan; add all the diced vegetables and the tomato, and sauté for a few minutes. Stir in the remaining ingredients, except the salt and pepper, and cook slowly until the mixture is moist but not runny. Remove from the heat and season to taste.

Make the port sauce by reducing the stock until thickish and concentrated. In a separate pan, reduce the port to a thick syrup, being careful not to burn it! Combine the stock and the port reduction.

Remove the skins from the potatoes, cut into wedges and deep-fry in hot oil until brown and crispy. Keep warm.

Using a sharp knife, stab all over the skin of the duck breasts. Heat a ridged grill pan until very hot, add a little olive oil and fry the breasts, skin side down. Transfer to a rack on a baking sheet and roast at 180 °C, checking after 3–4 minutes. The juices should run slightly pink when the breast is pierced and the meat should yield to fingertip pressure. Reheat the ratatouille. Reheat the sauce and whisk in the butter.

To serve, fill an egg-frying ring with ratatouille and place in the centre of a plate. Press down and top with half a duck breast, sliced. Arrange the potato wedges around the ring and drizzle with the sauce. Remove the ring. Repeat with 3 more plates. Wine pairing: This dish calls for KWV's seductive Reserve Merlot.

Serves 4

SWEET FRENCH TOAST WITH POACHED PEARS AND VAN DER HUM™ CUSTARD

John Jackson's favourite herbs add fragrant flavour to an old-fashioned dessert that is back in vogue.

SYRUP
250 ml (1 cup) hot water
250 ml (1 cup) white wine
125 ml (½ cup) white sugar
1 cinnamon stick
4 sprigs mint
2 lavender flowers
2 rose geranium leaves
4 lemon verbena leaves
2–4 firm ripe pears, peeled, halved lengthwise, cored and seeded

FOR THE CUSTARD
250 ml (1 cup) milk
3 eggs
125 ml (½ cup) sugar
50 ml (3 T plus 1 t) Van der Hum™ liqueur

FRENCH TOAST
4 thickly cut (1.5 cm) slices white bread
250 ml (1 cup) pouring cream
2 large eggs
100 g white sugar
50 g butter for frying

lavender flowers, rose geranium and lemon verbena leaves for garnishing
berries for garnishing

Poach the pears: Combine the syrup ingredients, except the pears, and bring to a simmer, stirring to dissolve the sugar. Add the pear halves and simmer gently until just tender. Cool in the syrup.

Make the custard: Whisk together the milk, eggs and sugar, transfer to the top of a double boiler and whisk over heat until the custard thickens. Transfer the pan to a large bowl of iced water to cool the custard. Stir in the liqueur.

For the toast, use a scone cutter to cut four rounds of bread from the slices. Whisk the cream until it starts to thicken, then whisk in the eggs and sugar. Soak the bread rounds in the egg mixture just until the egg has been absorbed. Heat the butter and fry the bread on both sides until puffed and golden brown.

To serve, divide the custard between four dessert bowls, place a round of French toast in the centre and top with one or two pear halves. Garnish with flowers, leaves and berries.

Serves 4

THE COTTON CLUB CAFÉ

There's usually some appealing four-legged orphan browsing its way around the gardens of the Cotton Club – I have seen baby warthog and small duiker during my visits to this oasis, popular local meeting place and informal restaurant for travellers driving between Phalaborwa and Hoedspruit. There are certain to be two-legged youngsters tumbling around the lawns as well, as this is an ideal family destination. Adjoining the fascinating Bombyx Mori Silk production operation, Ivory Room and Gallery – where we found plenty to interest visitors of all ages – the Cotton Club served up a substantial brunch that set us up for the rest of the day.

Duiker sometimes take refuge in this garden

LEFT: Charlotte Hunt, a versatile restaurateur with tales to tell
RIGHT: Alfresco breakfasts are on the menu

You will find the Cotton Club Café on the 24 Degrees South Country Estate, off the R531, not far from Hoedspruit. It is an integral part of the Bombyx Mori Silk operation (see Activities and Attractions, page 154), and is in an excellent position to offer travellers teas and delectable light meals as they take in Lowveld attractions like the Khamai Reptile Park. Silkworms, snakes and spiders offer game viewing of a different kind – and there are fewer restrictions involved!

Set in attractive shady gardens, against a distant mauve backdrop of the Blyde River Canyon, the restaurant is the most inviting spot to chill and to drink good coffee. Visitors have a choice of alfresco dining, or they can sit at sturdy wooden tables and chairs inside the restaurant, which has a high thatched roof.

Restaurateur Charlotte Hunt and her little team present a menu of tasty, contemporary dishes that focus on simple seasonal ingredients. Choices range from pasta options to substantial salads, from Charlotte's chicken and leek pie to ostrich kebabs, from burgers to vegetarian quiche.

There are a few tempting desserts and bakes, and items are reasonably priced, which makes the Cotton Club a popular venue for catered functions of all kinds.

In fact, catering is Charlotte's forte, as she has not only organised meals for former President Nelson Mandela, but has catered for cocktail functions and launches for some of South Africa's top political personalities, between starting up restaurants at important tourist sites and in city centres.

CHARLOTTE'S GRILLED QUAILS

Team this piquant starter with a small portion of Mediterranean salad, such as red pepper and black olives, or rocket with spring onion.

4 dressed quails
juice of 1 lemon
about 45 ml (3 T) olive oil
8 sage leaves
2 cloves garlic, peeled and halved
1 small red chilli, seeded and chopped
30 ml (2 T) balsamic vinegar
30 ml (2 T) brown sugar
small handful finely chopped rosemary needles
salt and ground black pepper
30 ml (2 T) chopped parsley
lemon slices to serve

Split each bird through the breastbone, using a sharp knife. Arrange in a single layer in a shallow dish. Combine the lemon juice, oil, sage, garlic, chilli, vinegar, sugar and rosemary, and mix well. Season with salt and pepper, and pour over the quails. Marinate for 30 minutes, turning the birds halfway through. Preheat the grill.

Transfer the birds, skin side up, to an oiled grill tray and grill for about 5 minutes on each side or until just cooked through. Sprinkle with parsley and serve with lemon slices and a seasonal salad.

Serves 4

THREE-CHEESE POLENTA WITH TOMATO SAUCE

This appetising vegetarian dish calls for a simple green salad on the side.

15 ml (1 T) salt
300 g coarse-grained polenta
75 g butter

TOMATO SAUCE
45 ml (3 T) olive oil
2 cloves garlic, crushed
15 g rosemary needles, roughly chopped
1 x 800 g can tomatoes
salt and ground black pepper
1 handful basil leaves, torn
200 g Gorgonzola cheese, cubed
250 g ricotta cheese
100 g Parmesan, coarsely grated

Bring 1,5 litres of water to the boil in a large, heavy-based saucepan and add the salt. Add the polenta in a thin stream, stirring vigorously. Reduce the heat immediately to a simmer. Stir continuously for a minute, then allow the polenta to bubble gently for 40 minutes, stirring every few minutes. Remove from the heat and stir in the butter. Pour the polenta into a shallow, greased baking tray and leave to cool.

Meanwhile, make the tomato sauce: heat the oil, add the garlic and cook gently until light brown. Add half of the rosemary, then stir in the tomatoes, crushing them with a fork. Season to taste, then simmer, stirring occasionally, until the sauce has reduced and thickened. Stir in the basil leaves.

Preheat the oven to 180 °C. Turn out the polenta and carefully slice the slab horizontally. Spoon half of the tomato sauce onto the base of the baking dish and cover with one half of the polenta. Season lightly, then scatter over the Gorgonzola cheese. Dot with the ricotta, and sprinkle with half of the Parmesan and the remaining rosemary. Top with the remaining polenta, pour over the rest of the tomato sauce and sprinkle with the rest of the Parmesan. Bake for about 30 minutes, and leave to rest for 10 minutes before slicing and serving.

Wine pairing: Serve this robust dish with a full-bodied red, such as KWV Pinotage.

Serves 6

COTTON CLUB PLUM TART

A classic autumn dessert that brings out the best in ripe, red plums.

PASTRY
500 ml (2 cups) flour
60 ml (4 T) icing sugar, sifted
2 ml (½ t) salt
180 g butter, cubed
15–30 ml (1–2 T) iced water

FILLING
4–6 plums, stoned and each cut into 6 wedges
3 eggs
125 ml (½ cup) castor sugar
30 ml (2 T) plain flour
90 g butter, melted and lightly browned

For the pastry combine the flour, icing sugar and salt and place in the bowl of a food processor. Add the butter and process until the mixture resembles coarse crumbs. Add enough iced water to make a firm dough. Roll out on a floured board until the pastry is 3 mm thick, then gently press into a greased 23 cm diameter tart tin and freeze for 30 minutes.

Preheat the oven to 180 °C. Remove the pastry from the freezer, line with baking paper and bake blind for about 8 minutes until a pale golden colour.

Arrange the fruit, skin side down, on the pastry case. Whisk the eggs and castor sugar together until thick and pale. Stir in the flour and melted butter. Pour the egg mixture evenly over the plums and bake the tart for 30–40 minutes until golden and the custard has set in the centre.

Serves 8

UMLANI BUSHCAMP

Right across the Lowveld sunset drinks are savoured in magical surroundings and nowhere better than on Umlani's bar deck overlooking the riverbed. On the far bank, wildlife paraded past in a dream sequence as we sipped exceptional sauvignon blanc. Heading the procession was a family of baboons, two youngsters cavorting to the gallery as they brought up the rear. Buck and buffalo followed in sedate single file as a giant full moon leapt up from behind marula trees, bathing the scene in a golden light, while intermittent roars from a male lion added the appropriate background sound.

Moonrise behind the Marula trees

Umlani in the Timbavati Private Nature Reserve perches serenely on the banks of the Nhlaralumi riverbed. Round thatched-roof huts enclose guests in Shangaan style, with only reeds and mosquito netting between occupants and nocturnal visitors. Hurricane lamps light both huts and paths outside, and the absence of fences adds a frisson of excitement to one's visit.

There's little doubt that some places reflect the spirit of the people who live – and have lived – there: at Umlani the passion exuded by past and present residents embraces those who are drawn here.

The camp was built by Marco and Marie-Louise Schiess, who laboured alongside their Shangaan workers to erect this 'place of rest'. They opened in 1989 with two huts, offering guided walking trails for adventurous visitors.

Although the camp has expanded over the years, rustic simplicity has been well maintained, augmented by a philosophy centred on sustainability – this long before the term became the buzzword it is today.

Gauteng couple Don and Nina Scott, aeronautical engineer and marketing director respectively, visited Umlani regularly for more than a decade as an antidote to their high-powered life.

The call of the wilderness intensified and in 2002 they took over management of Umlani. Here Nina – renowned as a gourmet hostess – faced a bush kitchen with waist-high walls, where honey badgers and hyenas competed as to which would carry off the largest share of anything edible every night. The badger probably won, as it learned to open the oven door ...

Nina and staff prepare a sophisticated supper in a basic kitchen

Don, meanwhile, met a series of challenges not remotely aeronautical. Yet the quality of warm hospitality that guests frequently comment on never diminished, and the high standard of cuisine was reflected in the results attained by Umlani in the 2005 Bush Banquet Challenge. They entered jointly with Alan McSmith Safaris and scooped first places in three categories, taking home the Tammy Trophy.

Umlani caters for a maximum of 16 guests, so that game drives, bush walks and campfire dinners are kept both exclusive and personal. This is a destination for those seeking the essence of the African wilderness.

EAST AFRICAN CHICKEN WITH COUSCOUS

A delicious dish from the continent's east coast but one that is influenced by ingredients from all over Africa. Replace palm sugar with soft brown sugar if necessary.

peanut oil
8 chicken thighs, skin left on, but excess fat removed
30 ml (2 T) whole cumin seeds
1 onion, chopped
1 clove garlic, crushed
5 ml (1 t) tomato purée or to taste
1 small red chilli, finely shredded, seeded if liked
600 ml (1½ x 400 ml cans) coconut milk
15 ml (1 T) palm sugar
juice of ½ lemon
20 ml (1½ T) smooth peanut butter
salt and ground black pepper
15 ml (1 T) desiccated coconut
1 small bunch fresh coriander, coarsely chopped
500 ml (2 cups) couscous
olive oil
sliced almonds, lightly toasted
flat-leaf parsley, chopped

Heat a tablespoon of peanut oil and brown the chicken, in two batches if necessary, on both sides. Remove from the pan. In a small dry pan cook the cumin seeds until they just start to smoke, then place in a mortar and pound until fine.

In a large heavy-based pot heat a little peanut oil, add the onion and garlic, and fry until the onion is transparent. Add the tomato purée, chilli and cumin, and cook, stirring for 1 minute. Add the chicken and pour over the coconut milk. Stir in the palm sugar, lemon juice and peanut butter, making sure the peanut butter dissolves in the liquid in the pot. Season to taste with salt and black pepper. Bring the mixture to the boil, reduce the heat, cover and simmer for about 40 minutes.

When the chicken is tender, stir in the coconut and check the seasoning.

Stir in the coriander and serve over the couscous.

While the chicken is cooking, prepare the couscous according to the package instructions. When the grains have been fluffed up, season and stir through enough olive oil just to moisten.

Scatter over the almonds and chopped parsley.

Serves 4

MOZAMBICAN PORK SOSATIES WITH CHORIZO

Lowvelders enjoy the fact that Mozambique is close enough for weekends by the sea. They also relish the country's spicy Portuguese-inspired cuisine.

800 g pork fillet
3 cloves garlic
20 ml (1 heaped T) Portuguese sweet paprika powder
4 bay leaves, 1 crushed, 3 whole
250 ml (1 cup) Portuguese olive oil
125 ml (½ cup) fresh lemon juice
sea salt and white pepper
1 green pepper
1 red pepper
1 Portuguese chorizo sausage
stoned black olives (optional)
handful flat-leaf parsley
wooden sosatie sticks, soaked in water

Cut the pork fillet into cubes about 2.5 cm square.

Thinly slice one garlic clove and smash the remaining two with the flat side of a large knife. In a glass or non-aluminium container, combine the garlic, paprika, bay leaves, oil and lemon juice, and season generously.

Add the pork, cover and marinate for at least 12 hours in a cool place or in the fridge.

Cut both peppers into flat pieces similar in size to the pork, and slice the chorizo thinly.

Remove the meat from the marinade, reserve the marinade, and skewer cubes onto sosatie sticks, alternating with peppers, sliced chorizo and olives, if using.

Grill the sosaties over medium to hot coals, basting several times with the reserved marinade. Cook for 15–20 minutes or until the meat is cooked through, but do not overcook. Garnish with chopped parsley and serve with chickpea salad (see page 66). Wine pairing: Offering accessible, enjoyable drinking, KWV Laborie Merlot/Cabernet Sauvignon blend will make an agreeable companion to these sosaties.

Serves 4

LABORIE
CABERNET SAUVIGN

CHICKPEA SALAD WITH CORIANDER

Unusual side salad that would make a good partner to most barbecued meat and poultry.

2 x 400 g cans chickpeas, drained, rinsed and drained again
1 small onion, chopped
1 large handful fresh coriander leaves, coarsely chopped
2 hard-boiled eggs, peeled and coarsely chopped
80 ml (⅓ cup) fresh lemon juice
160 ml (⅔ cup) Portuguese olive oil
sea salt and white pepper

Combine all the ingredients, except the salt and pepper, and mix gently. Season to taste and serve with the pork sosaties.

CHOCOLATE AND HAZELNUT TORTE WITH MASCARPONE

Nina enjoys surprising guests with this sophisticated dessert that had its origins in the city.

500 g hazelnuts
500 g dark chocolate (preferably Belgian), broken into pieces
500 g castor sugar
500 g unsalted butter, softened
12 eggs
mascarpone
brandied orange peel or fresh berries to garnish

Preheat the oven to 150 °C. Line a 25 cm loose-bottomed cake tin with buttered greaseproof paper. Roast the hazelnuts in the preheated oven for about 20 minutes until the skins become crisp and the nuts begin to colour. Remove the nuts from the oven, wrap in a tea towel and rub gently to remove the skins, then chop coarsely. Melt the chocolate in a bowl over simmering water. Do not stir!

Beat the sugar and butter until fluffy. Slowly add the melted chocolate. Mix in the eggs one by one, then add the chopped hazelnuts. Spoon the mixture into the prepared tin and bake for 40–50 minutes. Turn off the heat and leave the torte in the oven for a further 30 minutes. To serve, garnish torte slices with orange peel or berries, and add a tablespoon of mascarpone on the side.

Serves 12

KUNAME RIVER LODGE

Moving west from the Kruger National Park towards the Drakensberg escarpment, the vegetation becomes verdant, the trees taller ... Driving into the car park at Kuname was like entering a forest glade dominated by a huge Weeping Boer-bean, with Fever trees and Wild Figs, Jackalberrys and Marulas crowding in from the sides. Our initial impression of this mountain retreat was further strengthened by the design, the abundance of stone and the timber used to create this riverside lodge. But when it came to the cuisine, our taste buds revelled in traditional African flavours, given gourmet contemporary treatment by an innovative chef.

Verdant vegetation of the Edeni Reserve

Executive chef Hanroe Erasmus celebrates indigenous cuisine

Kuname lies off the R36 to Tzaneen, some 19 km from the Strydom Tunnel.

This small, exclusive lodge boasts an enviable position, built on several levels up the banks of the Kuvjename River. It occupies a lush environment within the Edeni Game Reserve, where trees are tall and sturdy, not having had to contend with elephant appetites until fairly recently.

The Big Five and many more can be seen on twice-daily game drives, and guests can also take walking trails where twitchers can look out for more than 250 species of birdlife that have been recorded on this conservancy.

Stone walls, thatched roofs and timbered interiors combine to induce an Alpine ambience, although the uniquely African panorama from the windows soon dispels that notion.

Dark panelling, attractive blinds and snowy linen make for agreeable contrasts in the bedrooms. Wooden decks feature open-air baths as well as showers, both with memorable vistas.

The Premier Suite, a retreat for romantics, goes one step further with its large, freestanding bath, set among a forest of ferns in a private tree-filled garden. Two family cottages complete the accommodation.

The lounge and dining room areas lead to decks and bomas that descend the riverbanks, each offering unique views. One even features an inviting rock pool.

Guests dine well at Kuname, whether relishing a barbecue on the deck, dinner in the boma or a meal around the indoor dining table.

Talented executive chef Hanroe Erasmus is not only enthusiastic about creating memorable meals, but is one of the few chefs in the area who makes a point of including heritage ingredients and regional dishes in his repertoire. When compiling the menu for Kuname's entry into the 2005 Bush Banquet Challenge, he turned to the small Sotho community living at the foot of the Drakensberg for inspiration. Sotho staff members of the lodge were enthusiastic assistants, obtaining ingredients for a feast that starred native ingredients seldom seen on game lodge tables.

Hanroe's 'Forgotten Africa' menu looked and tasted impressive, winning Kuname River Lodge places in several categories in the Silver Category. A few of his recipes follow.

WILD PUMPKIN AND MARULA NUT SOUP

The Marula tree is one of the best-known indigenous trees of the region, and one of the most useful. The fruits are favoured by birds and mammals, including humans, who use it to make delicious jellies and a potent alcoholic drink.

olive oil
75 g fresh root ginger, finely chopped
4 Granny Smith apples, peeled, cored and cubed
300 g Marula nuts or macadamia nuts, lightly roasted
about 2.5 kg wild pumpkin or butternut squash, peeled and cubed
15 ml (1 T) mixed spice
1 litre (4 cups) vegetable stock, plus extra for thinning
salt and ground black pepper
home-made yoghurt to serve
additional roasted Marula nuts to serve

In a large, deep, heavy-based pot, heat a little oil, sauté the ginger for 2 minutes, add the apples and stir for a minute, then add the nuts and stir to coat with oil. Stir in half the pumpkin, then add the remainder, along with the spice and stock. Bring to a boil, reduce the heat and simmer the mixture until the pumpkin is very tender. You may need to add more stock. Cool a little, then blend the soup in batches until very smooth. Reheat and season to taste. Top each serving with a dollop of home-made yoghurt and additional nuts, if wanted. Accompany the soup with bulrush bread (see page 72) on the side.

Serves 6

BULRUSH BREAD

Bulrush is more generally used for thatching, mats and baskets. As few cooks will have access to this unusual flour ground by Sotho communities, substitute whole wheat or rye flour.

325 g cake flour
200 g bread flour
125 g Bulrush flour
1 packet instant yeast
5 ml (1 t) salt
5 ml (1 t) castor sugar
30 g unsalted butter
125 ml (½ cup) water
250 ml (1 cup) milk

Sieve all the dry ingredients together into a large mixing bowl. Rub in the butter with your fingers. Combine the water and milk and heat in the microwave oven for 45 seconds. Slowly mix this into the flour mixture with a wooden spoon. Transfer the dough to a floured surface and knead until it is soft and elastic. Place in a buttered bowl and cover with plastic wrap. Leave in a warm place to rise for about 30 minutes, then softly knead it down. Shape into a loaf and place on a baking tray. Leave in a warm place for 15 minutes, then bake at 210 °C for about 45 minutes.

AFRICAN POLENTA

Kuname uses this as an accompaniment to various meat dishes.

1 litre (4 cups) full-cream milk
1 litre (4 cups) water
100 g butter
15 ml (1 T) salt
500 g super maize meal
100 g grated Parmesan cheese

Combine all the ingredients, except the maize and Parmesan, in a large, heavy-based pot and bring to the boil, stirring occasionally. When the mixture is bubbling slowly, add the maize, while whisking vigorously. Let the mixture bubble until it has a thick porridge-like consistency, then stir in the Parmesan. Transfer to a large, buttered baking tray, level the top and leave to cool. When firm and set, cut into rectangles or other shapes, then fry until lightly browned.

Serves 8 or more

GRILLED KUDU FILLET WITH SPICY CITRUS SAUCE

Chef Erasmus prefers to use kudu for this Lowveld main course that also stars local citrus, but beef can replace the venison if preferred.

ground black pepper
50 ml olive oil
1 whole kudu fillet (about 2.5 kg), trimmed
salt to taste

CITRUS SAUCE
1 litre (4 cups) freshly squeezed orange juice
15 ml (1 T) lemon juice
3 whole star anise
3 whole cloves
1 whole cinnamon stick
10 peppercorns
pinch salt
5 ml (1 t) cornflour

Start a day ahead. Grind a generous amount of black pepper into the olive oil, mix well, then rub this into the fillet. Sprinkle with a little salt, then wrap the fillet tightly in plastic wrap and refrigerate for up to 24 hours.

Meanwhile, make the sauce: Combine all the ingredients, except the cornflour, in a saucepan, bring to the boil, reduce the heat and leave to simmer until the liquid has reduced by half. Remove from the heat and strain. Return to the pan, bring to a simmer, and thicken with the cornflour, mixed to a paste with a little water, stirring constantly.

Remove the meat from the fridge at least 2 hours before grilling. Place under a very hot grill and brown well on all sides. Leave to rest for 20 minutes before slicing into medallions and serving with the citrus sauce.

Serves 8

BROWN IVORY ICE CREAM WITH MACADAMIA PRALINE

Brown Ivory is an indigenous evergreen tree found across much of Africa. It bears abundant fruit that is popular with humans and baboons, game and birds alike. The sugar content can be as high as 30%. The fruit is also used to make a potent alcoholic drink. In Northern Sotho it is called Mogokgomo. Substitute dates if necessary.

4 egg yolks
75 g castor sugar
250 g Brown Ivory fruit (or dates), stoned and chopped
1 litre (4 cups) cream

MACADAMIA PRALINE
50 g butter
60 g golden syrup
45 ml cake flour
75 g castor sugar
80 g macadamia nuts, roughly chopped

Whisk the egg yolks and sugar until pale and creamy. Combine the chopped fruit and cream in a heavy-based saucepan, and bring slowly to the boil, stirring continuously. Remove from the heat and pour slowly onto the egg mixture, while whisking. Return the mixture to the saucepan, place over low heat, and whisk continuously until the mixture thickens to a custard. Transfer to an ice cream machine and churn for 2 hours.
Transfer to a container and freeze for about 8 hours. If you do not have an ice cream machine, freeze the custard in a bowl, whisking every hour to aerate the ice cream.
To make the praline, melt the butter in a small, heavy saucepan and add the syrup, stirring until the syrup has melted.
Remove the pan from the heat and stir in the remaining ingredients, mixing well.
Quickly transfer the mixture to a well-greased baking tray, and spread out evenly.
Bake for 15 minutes at 180 °C until golden brown. Cool for 5 minutes, then break or cut into desired shapes. If too hard, return to a 120 °C oven for a few minutes.
Serve scoops of ice cream topped with shards of macadamia praline.
Serves 6–8

LION SANDS PRIVATE GAME RESERVE

Not only the guests but also the wildlife seem to be particularly relaxed around the two Lion Sands lodges. While driving the last few kilometres to the gate, we were surrounded on all sides by duiker, impala, nyala and the usually shy bushbuck. They looked at us, twitched an ear or two and ambled on unperturbed, which made for an appealing approach to this charming gem on the banks of the Sabie. Given its unique riverside position, River Lodge makes an ideal destination for a memorable bush experience in comfortable, informal surroundings. The second option is Ivory Lodge, a small camp offering luxurious exclusivity.

Sunset over the Sabie

This privately owned game reserve within the Sabi Sand Game Reserve boasts a history that merges adventure with conservation, passion with endurance. The reserve is run by the More family, who are aware of being privileged custodians and are delighted to be able to share its attractions with guests from South Africa and across the globe.

The More brothers' great-grandfather purchased 4 000 ha of wilderness bordering the Kruger National Park early in the 20th century and soon exchanged hunting for conservation, a tradition still maintained today. The family built two camps with basic facilities on the banks of the Sabie River and opened in 1978.

The new millennium started disastrously as floods transformed the river into a raging torrent, which overflowed, rising above roof height at the camps.

Nicholas and Robert More, together with their father, not only rebuilt River Lodge, but went on to create the ultra-luxurious Ivory Lodge. This lodge consists of private and spacious contemporary suites, featuring uncluttered, striking décor. The result is timeless elegance not often seen in the bush.

Guests at both lodges can augment game drives with morning and full-moon walks, and excursions that focus on the hippos and crocodiles lurking in the Sabie River. Another unique option is to book a night in one of two tree houses: these are fully equipped bush bedrooms, one perched high in an ancient Leadwood tree, and the other in a century-old Jackalberry. Both offer an extraordinary African experience.

Executive chef Janine Hobbs adds innovative twists to classic fare

Those who prefer to keep their feet on the ground will find the thatched suites at River Lodge comfortable and well equipped, with air-conditioning, tea and coffee facilities, a well-stocked bar fridge and sensible reading lamps.

Enthusiastic and well-qualified executive chef Janine Hobbs presents delectable buffets and set menus of contemporary fare given innovative touches – as in colourful starters such as garlicky black mushrooms topped with haloumi, or cherry tomatoes dressed with tequila mayonnaise. Some excellent wines, worthy of partnering these feasts, are housed in a cool cellar beneath the lounge area of Ivory Lodge.

RIVER LODGE BREAKFAST SPECIAL

Chef Hobbs has combined two classic egg dishes and added South African flavour with minced meat and chutney to create a hearty start to long days in the bush.

4 spinach leaves
45 ml (3 T) cream
½ medium onion, coarsely chopped
2 cubes Danish feta cheese
160 g impala mince
fruity chutney
2 ml (½ t) paprika
salt and ground black pepper
2 eggs
2 English muffins
hollandaise sauce

Remove the white stalks from the spinach and chop the leaves coarsely. Place the spinach, cream, onion and feta in a saucepan, bring to a simmer and cook, stirring occasionally, until the spinach and onion are just tender. Heat a frying pan and sauté the mince until browned, then add chutney to taste, season the mixture with paprika, salt and pepper, and continue cooking for a few minutes. In a separate pan, poach the eggs in simmering water. While they are cooking, split the muffins and toast until golden. On each of two warmed plates, place the toasted muffin halves. Divide the mince between the two, covering the muffins. Top with half the creamed spinach on each plate, and finish with a poached egg. Drizzle the eggs with warm hollandaise and serve immediately.

Serves 2

RIVER LODGE MINTED CUCUMBER AND YOGHURT SOUP

When the mercury soars and humidity envelopes the Lowveld, this makes a refreshing start to a meal.

2 English cucumbers, diced
1 medium onion, diced
15 ml (1 T) butter
250 ml (1 cup) water
300 g Greek yoghurt
bottled mint jelly
salt and white pepper

Combine the cucumber, onion and butter in a medium saucepan, place over medium heat and sauté the vegetables, stirring continuously. Add the water, bring to a simmer and cook until the cucumber is tender. Cool the mixture before transferring it to a blender or processor. Add the yoghurt and mint jelly to taste, then blend the mixture until fairly smooth. Season to taste, then chill well before serving in chilled bowls.

Serves up to 8

ROCKET, PEAR, BEET AND GOAT'S CHEESE SALAD

If you don't want to deep-fry, simply slice the chèvre and add it to the salad without the crumbs.

2 firm, ripe pears, cut lengthwise into thin wedges
125 ml (½ cup) vinaigrette dressing
1 chilli-coated log of goat's milk cheese (chèvre)
dried breadcrumbs
oil for deep-frying
1 pillow packet rocket leaves, washed and spun dry
4 medium beetroot, cooked, peeled and sliced

Grill or braai the pear wedges under a preheated grill or on an oiled grid until just tender. Remove from the heat, pour over the dressing, and leave to cool. Roll the cheese into little balls, coat in the breadcrumbs and deep-fry. Scatter the rocket leaves over the base of a serving platter. Top with the sliced beets, grilled pears, and cheese balls. Sprinkle over the dressing from the pears.

Serves 4 as a starter

ROASTED SWEET POTATO, BANANA, LITCHI AND GORGONZOLA SALAD

Here's a salad from River Lodge that combines African produce and Lowveld specialities with the sophistication of exotic cheese. If made in winter, canned litchis can be used.

6 medium sweet potatoes, peeled and cubed
80 g butter, melted
10 ml (2 t) brown sugar
1 banana, thickly sliced
lemon juice
10 litchis, peeled and pitted
100 g Gorgonzola cheese, crumbled
fresh herbs to garnish (optional)

Place the cubed sweet potato in a shallow ovenproof dish. Pour over the butter, sprinkle over the sugar and toss to coat. Bake at 190 °C until tender but not very soft. Cool to room temperature. Toss the banana in a little lemon juice. Assemble the salad with sweet potato on the base, and litchi and banana arranged on top. Sprinkle with the cheese and garnish with herbs, if using. Drizzle around with basil oil if wanted.

Serves 8 as a side dish

RIVER LODGE GUAVA AND WHITE CHOCOLATE-SPIKED MUFFINS

Guavas grow abundantly in Lowveld orchards, ripening in winter and spring. Amarula Cream™ is a popular liqueur made from the Marula fruit that grows wild in the region.

300 g cake flour
10 ml (2 t) baking powder
150 g castor sugar
1 egg
5 ml (1 t) vanilla extract
225 ml milk
50 g butter, melted
3 guavas, peeled, seeded and diced
75 g white chocolate, diced
50 ml (3 generous T) Amarula Cream™

Preheat the oven to 200 °C. Cut 8 x 15 cm diameter circles of greaseproof paper and use to line the cups of a muffin tin.

Sift the flour and baking powder together in a large bowl, and stir in the castor sugar.

In a smaller bowl, whisk together the egg, vanilla extract, milk and melted butter.

Stir the egg mixture into the dry ingredients, along with the guava, chocolate and Amarula Cream™, being careful not to over-mix.

Spoon the batter into the muffin cups and bake for about 30 minutes or until well risen and firm to the touch.

Makes 8

RISSINGTON INN

A purple-crested loerie skittered across the canopies of flowers capping venerable frangipani trees, sending a shower of perfumed petals to earth. Walking under these giant specimens on my way to breakfast felt like treading a bridal path rather than heading for a table on the deep, tiled stoep that serves as an alfresco dining area. Once the menu was proffered, the promise of fine fare from the renowned Rissington kitchen required my full attention, and I dithered between an order of Croque Monsieur or Popeye's spinach, feta and avocado omelette as the preferred start to the day.

Fragrant frangipani blossoms carpet the path to Rissington

Rustic comfort in Rissington's dining area

A number of features help to explain why this inn enjoys such high occupancy. When friendly service and consistently good culinary standards are combined with affordability, the result is a winning formula, underscored by bookings from travellers across the globe.

After just a few hours at Rissington Inn, it's easy to understand why this country lodge hotel has garnered an impressive number of awards.

The inn occupies the site of a former tobacco farm. A century ago the working farm was neighbour to the property of a larger-than-life Lowveld character: game ranger Harry Wolhuter was creating legends through feats like his famous – and successful – hand-to-hand combat with two lions. Today the former farmstead and drying barn seem comfortable in their hospitality role, although their air of serene maturity is tinged with hints of an intriguing past.

The en suite rooms and suites are set in 10 acres of colourful, shady gardens, many of which enjoy sweeping views over the Sabie River valley.

Its position outside Hazyview makes Rissington ideal for stopovers, either en route to or from the game reserves. Here guests are free to fill the hours as they wish, with breakfast being served all morning, and dinner from early until late.

Rissington marked its 10th anniversary in 2005 by being awarded four stars by the Grading Council and gaining gold from the Diners Club for their wine list. The hotel was also chosen as a Michelin South Africa Coup de Coeur Preferred Establishment, given only to those few places that 'steal the hearts' of tough inspectors. Chris Harvie and his team maintain high standards of hospitality that are an example to the industry.

The menu at Rissington – larger than one would expect, given the high gastronomic standard – tempts with contemporary dishes augmented by a few classics, all well cooked and attractively presented.

Along with the recipes that follow, the apple and whisky soup and the smoked trout cheesecake come highly recommended. The wine list is a delight to peruse. Rissington Inn was a runner-up in the Silver Category of the 2005 Bush Banquet in the Best Kitchen, Best Food and Best Food and Wine pairing sections.

RISSINGTON PAN-FRIED TROUT WITH MUSTARD TARRAGON SAUCE

Trout come from Dullstroom, a region of numerous streams, some way to the east of Hazyview. Ingredient quantities can be varied to taste, and can be doubled to make two servings.

butter
1 fresh trout, filleted but not skinned
dry white wine
ground black pepper
±1 t (5 ml) creamed mustard
fresh tarragon leaves and dill tops
cream
salt (optional)
prepared creamed spinach to accompany

In a large pan, melt a knob of butter, add the trout, flesh side down, and heat through. Add a little wine, grind over black pepper, and stir in the mustard. Sprinkle over the herbs, cover the pan and cook the fish over low heat until just cooked through. Remove the skin from the fillet, then remove the fish from the pan and keep warm. Add sufficient cream to the pan to make a fairly thin sauce, and heat through. Taste, and add salt if necessary.

To serve, arrange the trout on top of a bed of spinach and top with the sauce.

Wine pairing: To enhance this fishy delight, pour a glass of KWV Reserve Sauvignon Blanc.

Serves 1

MOTHER-IN-LAW CURRIED CHICKEN

Mother-in-law spices, a curry-type mix, can be found on the spice shelves of large supermarkets.

25 ml (5 t) butter
25 ml (5 t) oil
2 medium onions, finely chopped
1.5 kg chicken on the bone, cut into serving portions
60 ml (4 T) mild curry powder
10 ml (2 t) ground coriander
10 ml (2 t) mother-in-law spices
20 ml (4 t) turmeric
pinch ground cinnamon
125 ml (½ cup) raisins
pinch sugar
10 ml (2 t) salt
500 ml (2 cups) home-made chicken stock
125 ml (½ cup) cream
15 ml (1 T) cornflour
60 ml (4 T) brandy

Heat the butter and oil in a large, deep pan, add the onion and sauté until it starts to soften. Add the chicken pieces in batches, browning well on all sides. Transfer the chicken and onion to an ovenproof dish. Stir the spices, raisins, sugar and salt into the stock, then pour this over the chicken. Cover and bake at 160 °C for 1 hour or until the chicken is tender. Combine the cream, cornflour and brandy in a small saucepan, stirring until the mixture simmers and thickens. Pour the sauce over the chicken and return to the oven to heat through. Serve with rice and Rissington Banana Chutney.

Serves 6

RISSINGTON BANANA CHUTNEY

Van der Hum™ is a South African liqueur made from naartjies (tangerines).

500 g dried cling peaches, marinated in Van der Hum™
rind of 1 lemon, cut into strips and marinated in Van der Hum™
500 g bananas
500 g dried dates
500 g seedless raisins
1 clove garlic, crushed
400 g sugar
1.5 litres (6 cups) vinegar
500 ml (2 cups) water
1 ml (pinch) ground cinnamon
15 ml (1 T) salt
1 ml (pinch) cayenne pepper

Mince all the fruit. Mix with the remaining ingredients and simmer in a saucepan, stirring occasionally, for 90 minutes or until thick. Bottle and seal immediately.

Makes about 2 litres

RISSINGTON GLAZED GAMMON

This timeless classic is popular with guests from countries around the world.

3.6–4.5 kg gammon
3 large onions
4 stalks celery
3 large carrots
2 turnips
2 parsnips
4 stalks parsley
2 bay leaves
15 peppercorns
300 ml (1¼ cups) cider vinegar
225 g soft brown sugar

GLAZE
150 g soft brown sugar
25 g soft brown breadcrumbs
10 ml (2 t) Dijon mustard
15 ml (1 T) cider vinegar

HERB MUSTARD SAUCE
2 eggs
60 g sugar
salt to taste
10 ml (2 t) mustard powder
125 ml (½ cup) white vinegar
10 ml (2 t) each chopped fresh spring onion, origanum and dill tops
5 ml (1 t) mustard seeds, crushed
125 ml (½ cup) sour cream

Start a day in advance. Scrub the gammon all over and soak for 24 hours in cold water.

Scrub the vegetables, cut into chunks and lay them in a thick layer in the bottom of a large pan or casserole. Add the parsley, bay leaves, peppercorns, vinegar and sugar. Lay the gammon on top, and cover with cold water. Bring to the boil and make a note of the time the first bubbles reach the surface.

Skim until the surface is clear, then cook steadily, keeping the water just below boiling point, for 20 minutes per 450 g. Allow the gammon to cool partially in its stock. An hour or so later, lift it out and remove the skin.

For the glaze, mix the sugar and breadcrumbs to a paste with the mustard and vinegar. Spread this all over the fatty surface of the gammon. Bake, uncovered, for 45 minutes at 180 °C, basting halfway through with a little vinegar. Leave for 15 minutes before carving.

Meanwhile, make the mustard sauce: Whisk the eggs, then beat in the sugar, salt and mustard. Slowly stir in the vinegar, then heat the mixture, stirring, until it thickens. Leave to cool before adding the herbs and mustard seeds. When ready to serve, stir in the sour cream. Serve warm as an accompaniment to the glazed ham.

Wine pairing: I would choose KWV's Cathedral Cellar Chardonnay, while others would prefer the KWV Pinotage.

Serves 12–16

CATHEDRAL
CELLAR

Vuyatela in the Djuma Game Reserve

Arrive at Vuyatela and delight in the difference … A fusion of township and bush architecture celebrates the new South Africa in zany, colourful style. Visitors are greeted by walls of zinc as well as stone that encompass lounge and dining areas vibrant with naïve township art and brilliant napery. Household names of South African favourites are given pride of place on cushion covers and tablecloths. A closer look at the magnificent tiered chandelier reveals ascending circles of Coca-Cola® bottles. Invited to enjoy 'bush television', guests are shown the large aquarium where local freshwater fish dart among aquatic plants.

Welcoming committee of one awaits guests' arrival

ABOVE LEFT: Starting life in Djuma Reserve
ABOVE RIGHT: The kitchen team hopes that guests bring keen appetites

Vuyatela is an eight-chalet lodge in Djuma Private Game Reserve, which is located in the Sabi Sand Game Reserve. Owned by the Moolman family, this 5-star lodge is one of a trio, the others being Djuma Bush Lodge which they built themselves and opened in 1994, and Galago Camp, which they acquired in 1999. This was also the year that Vuyatela opened, offering guests luxurious *kayas* with several unique features.

Living rooms have walls of wooden poles, the gaps packed with stones, while those of the adjacent bedroom suites are solid and ochre-coloured, adorned with designs painstakingly applied with toothbrushes.

Inside, mosaic work draws guests through an air-conditioned dressing room and bathroom to a reed-walled outside shower. Vervet monkeys are likely to eye you as you enjoy the plunge pool on your deck.

Facilities include a spa – dubbed the Rubbing Post – a gym, a library and Internet access. Djuma was the first game reserve in Africa to place permanent cameras at waterholes and on a mobile vehicle, giving Web surfers virtual game spotting at any time.

Game drives and bush walks that take in the Big Five can be further enhanced by sightings of seldom-seen animals, spotted by friendly, enthusiastic rangers who will join you later at table.

Simple, flavourful contemporary cuisine is served at Vuyatela, teamed with a good selection of wines, locally sourced. Their choice of wines for their Bush Banquet Challenge menu won them recognition in 2005.

Djuma's philosophy of active involvement in the community is well expressed at the N'wa Tumberi Day Care Centre in Utha, their neighbouring Shangaan village. Started by Jurie and Philippa in 1999 and supported by the reserve, their two daughters can be found in class there.

The reserve is one of a handful of South African destinations that may display the trademark of Fair Trade In Tourism South Africa, having met the stringent standards in tourism categories that include wages, working conditions, ethical business practice and respect for human rights and the environment.

As you dine under the stars – replicated nearer the ground with fairy lights strung through a giant marula tree – it's easy to agree with murmurs of 'Vuyatela', which means 'Come back again …'

DUCK AND LITCHI STIR-FRY

The distinctive flavour of Lowveld litchis adds an exotic dimension to the honeyed spices of this dish – use fresh litchis if you can get them.

2 large onions, sliced
1 x 1.8 kg duck, wingtips and oil gland removed
10 ml (2 t) salt
30 g honey
10 ml (2 t) crushed cumin
7 ml (1½ t) paprika
5 ml (1 t) cayenne pepper
45 ml (3 T) lemon juice
2.5 ml (½ t) ground cloves
3 leeks, well washed and cut into long strips
1 punnet mangetout peas, strings removed and cut into strips
1 x 565 g can litchis, drained, fruit diced and juice reserved
30 ml (2 T) Worcestershire sauce

Sprinkle the onion on the base of a roasting pan. Cut the duck in half lengthwise and place on the onion. Rub salt into the duck flesh. Combine the honey with the cumin, paprika, cayenne pepper, lemon juice and cloves, and mix to a paste, then rub this into the duck on all sides.

Roast the duck at 200 °C for ±1 hour, then remove from the oven and cool.

Remove the skin, place it on a rack over an ovenproof pan and crisp it in the oven. Cut the crisped skin into thin strips. Reserve the duck fat.

Remove the meat from the carcass; cut it into strips. Heat a little duck fat in a large pan or wok, add the leeks and peas, and stir-fry briefly. Add the reserved litchi juice and the Worcestershire sauce, and heat through. Add the duck meat and litchis, and stir gently until heated through. Garnish with the crisped skin and serve with rice. Wine suggestion: KWV Sauvignon Blanc or the Laborie sparkling Blanc de Noir.

Serves up to 10

VENISON BOBOTIE

This famous Cape classic was originally made with leftover roast mutton, but today beef mince is usually used. In the Lowveld, venison mince makes a tasty substitute.

15 ml (1 T) sunflower oil
15 ml (1 T) butter
1 kg venison mince
2 medium onions, chopped
5 ml (1 t) crushed garlic
5 ml (1 t) finely grated root ginger
25 ml (1½ T) medium curry powder
10 ml (2 t) ground turmeric
30 ml (2 T) smooth apricot jam
2 thickish slices day-old white bread, crusts removed
500 ml (2 cups) milk
2 eggs, lightly beaten
30 ml (2 T) fruity chutney
juice and grated rind of 1 lemon
salt and ground black pepper

TOPPING
3 eggs
375 ml (1½ cups) milk
5 ml (1 t) ground turmeric
about 5 bay leaves, preferably fresh

Heat the oil and butter together in a large, deep, heavy-based saucepan. Add the mince in batches, stirring to break up, and brown lightly. Remove with a slotted spoon and set aside. To the pan add the onion, garlic and ginger, and cook, stirring, until the onion has softened and coloured. Return the meat to the pan and stir in the curry powder, turmeric and apricot jam, and cook the mixture, stirring occasionally, until the mince is cooked through.

Meanwhile soak the bread in the milk, then crumble the bread and remove from any leftover milk. Remove the pan from the heat and cool a little. Mix the bread into the meat mixture, followed by the beaten eggs, chutney, lemon juice and rind. Season with salt and black pepper, and spoon the mixture into an ovenproof casserole dish. Level the top.

For the topping, beat the eggs with the milk, stir in the turmeric, then pour carefully over the top of the meat. Spike the bay leaves into the mixture at intervals, then bake for about 35 minutes at 190 °C until the custard topping has set.

Serve with poppadums, and coconut and radish sambal (see page 98).

Wine pairing here is easy: A good indigenous dish deserves a good indigenous wine, so try KWV Pinotage.

Serves 12

KWV
2003
PINOTAGE

COCONUT AND RADISH SAMBAL

This sambal makes an unusual addition to the usual bobotie accompaniments of yellow rice and tomato and onion salad.

500 ml (2 cups) shaved coconut
1 bunch freshly harvested radishes, washed, trimmed and sliced
125 ml (½ cup) white wine vinegar
125 ml (½ cup) white sugar
5 ml (1 t) salt

Toast the coconut in a frying pan over medium heat, ensuring that it does not catch. Dry the radish slices and place in a dish. Combine the vinegar, sugar and salt in a small pan and stir. Bring to a boil; simmer for 2 minutes. Cool. Pour the dressing over the radish slices and leave to cool completely. Stir in the coconut shavings.

CHURROS

I enjoyed these moreish morsels for breakfast at Vuyatela, but they would be good with coffee too.

500 ml (2 cups) water
125 g hard margarine
500 ml (2 cups) cake flour
2.5 ml (½ t) salt
4 eggs
500 ml (2 cups) oil for deep-frying
250 ml (1 cup) white sugar
10 ml (2 t) ground cinnamon

Bring the water to the boil in a large saucepan, add the margarine and bring back to the boil, stirring occasionally. Remove from the heat and add the flour and salt all at once, beating to a smooth paste with a wooden spoon. Cool slightly before beating in the eggs, one by one, until there is a sheen to the paste.
Transfer the dough to a piping bag with a star nozzle.
Heat the oil in a deep pan. Pipe the dough into the hot oil in long strips and deep-fry until golden.
Drain, then toss in the combined sugar and cinnamon and serve.
Serves up to 20

CHOCOLATE AND SWEET POTATO CAKE

This is a rich and popular item with guests at Vuyatela, many of whom don't guess that sweet potato makes an important ingredient.

180 g butter
360 g brown sugar
4 eggs
450 g cake flour
100 g cocoa powder
15 ml (1 T) baking powder
180 g dark chocolate, melted
400 g sweet potato, cooked, peeled and grated
400 ml buttermilk

GANACHE
20 ml (4 t) instant coffee powder
400 ml cream
300 g dark chocolate
120 g butter
strawberry jam to sandwich

Cream together the butter and brown sugar until smooth. Beat in the eggs, one by one. Sift together the flour, cocoa and baking powder, and fold into the creamed mixture. Fold in the melted chocolate, grated sweet potato and then the buttermilk, and mix well. Divide the batter between greased cake tins and bake at 180 °C for about 30 minutes or until a tester comes out clean. Cool on a wire rack.

Make the ganache by combining the coffee powder, cream, chocolate and butter in the top half of a double boiler. Heat over simmering water until the ingredients have melted to a smooth mixture, stirring occasionally. Cool.

Sandwich the cake layers with strawberry jam, then cover the top and sides with the chocolate ganache.

Serves 10

Garonga Safari Camp

Just when we seemed to have been driving through the Bushveld forever, a little sign on the right of the track pronounced: 'You are nearly there!' Soon after, we spied the curve of a rosy wall, its pinnacle a light-hearted take on a termite mound. Bernie was waiting for us, hand outstretched. Dust, distance and heat were forgotten as we were enveloped by friendliness. An Austrian couple had just exchanged wedding vows under the Jackalberry tree. Someone had scratched 'I love you' in the sand tray on the deck – a message not only appropriate to the occasion, but one that seemed to generate goodwill among all.

This well-placed sign keeps travellers on track

Chef Reineth Mkhatshwa has been in from the start

Garonga Safari Camp is located in the Greater Makalali Game Reserve, which lies northwest of Hoedspruit, off the R40 to Gravelotte.

This former cattle farm, also used for private hunting, was bought by Bernado Smith in 1996. Exchanging damp UK climes for the heat of the Lowveld, he set about returning the land to its Bushveld environment, building a small but luxurious camp, and dropping boundary fences so that Garonga could join the Makalali reserve. He opened for business a year later.

From the start, Garonga promised a holistic wildlife experience, allied to a flexible, relaxed itinerary for guests. Game drives can take in four of the Big Five that inhabit the reserve, or rangers can focus on smaller bush creatures. Walking, tracking and sleep-out excursions make memorable alternatives, offering more intimate wildlife encounters.

Before most of the top lodges installed spas, Garonga was – and still is – offering guests baths beneath the stars and aromatherapy sessions, with the emphasis on unwinding in a home-from-home environment. The help-yourself bar on the lounge deck emphasises the hospitable ambience of the camp.

The six tented suites combine dusky pink walls with canvas sides, front and roof, opening to decks where hammocks swing gently in the breeze. Sweeping views across the reserve are framed by Knobthorn trees. Inside the décor fuses Morocco with Makalali – alcoves in the walls provide storage, built-out shelves serve as bathroom seats, and indoor and outdoor showers add luxurious touches.

Good food is definitely on the menu at Garonga, with Bernie taking a keen interest in the cuisine, which changes seasonally. Guests dine at rustic tables made locally and sip well-chosen Cape wines. Well-cooked fare (including perfectly poached eggs, always a tell-tale item) is attractively plated and prettily garnished. Kitchen staff work under the watchful eye of head chef Reineth Mkhatshwa, who has been with the camp since it opened.

As Garonga consists of just six tents, it's easy to maintain an air of informal intimacy. But there's also a very luxurious honeymoon suite, complete with ebony four-poster and a private pool, to lure romantic couples of all ages.

OSTRICH CARPACCIO

Lean, flavourful ostrich meat makes a good alternative to beef and is a favourite with health-conscious diners and gourmets.

1.5 kg ostrich fillet
handful finely chopped rosemary needles
salt and freshly ground black pepper
30 ml (2 T) extra-virgin olive oil

BEETROOT MARMALADE
4 medium beetroot, scrubbed and trimmed
2 medium onions, chopped
60 ml (4 T) balsamic vinegar
60 ml (4 T) syrup from a jar of watermelon konfyt (preserves)

Leaving the fillet in one piece, coat the meat with the rosemary, salt and black pepper. Rub in the spices vigorously. Heat a frying pan until hot, add the oil and then the fillet, and sear for about 5 minutes until it has browned on all sides. Remove the meat from the pan and leave to rest for about 10 minutes before slicing very thinly. Arrange on a platter, garnish with fresh rosemary, and serve with beetroot marmalade.

For the marmalade, grate the beetroot coarsely. Combine with the rest of the ingredients in a small saucepan, bring to a boil, reduce the heat and simmer until the beetroot and onion are tender.

Serve at room temperature.

Serves 8 as part of a lunch buffet

THAI-STYLE BEEF AND GREEN PAWPAW SALAD

As you drive through the villages of Mpumalanga, you will see tall trees bearing bunches of pawpaws around their crowns outside many a small house. Orchards of this subtropical fruit can be glimpsed from the highways, as the area is a major producer of pawpaw and papino.

750 g beef fillet or rump steak
60 ml (4 T) light soy sauce
coarsely ground black pepper
olive oil
about 350 g green pawpaw, peeled and coarsely shredded
2 small, fresh green chillies, finely chopped, and seeded for a milder flavour
1 red pepper, seeded and thinly sliced (optional)
1 yellow pepper, seeded and thinly sliced
250 ml (1 cup) fresh lime juice
30 ml (2 T) Thai fish sauce
30 ml (2 T) soft brown sugar
1–2 cloves garlic, crushed
handful fresh mint leaves, coarsely chopped
1 packet mixed baby salad leaves
handful coriander leaves, stemmed

Trim the meat and remove any sinews. Combine the soy sauce with plenty of black pepper and enough olive oil to make a marinade, then marinate the beef for at least 30 minutes.

Meanwhile, combine the shredded pawpaw with the chillies and sliced peppers, and chill.

Make a dressing with the lime juice, fish sauce, sugar and garlic, stirring until the sugar has dissolved, then stir in the mint leaves.

Drain the meat from the marinade, and grill under a very hot, preheated grill until cooked on the outside but still very rare in the middle. Cool, then slice.

When ready to serve, arrange the salad greens on a platter or individual plates, and top with sliced beef. Spoon the pawpaw mixture over the beef, then scatter the coriander leaves over the top. Variation: If peppers are unavailable, tomato and onion are added, and the coriander replaced with rosemary.

Wine pairing: Team this Asian-style creation with KWV Chenin Blanc, or experiment with an off-dry fruity white or white blend.

Serves 2–4 depending on appetite

KWV

MIXED MELON SALAD WITH GINGER AND ALMONDS

This is a refreshing salad to counter the sticky heat of the Lowveld, and features local melons and preserved ginger, which is also cultivated in the region.

250 ml (1 cup) cubed, seedless, firm, ripe watermelon
250 ml (1 cup) cubed, seeded Ogen or winter melon (green fleshed)
250 ml (1 cup) cubed, seeded spanspek (cantaloupe or sweet melon)
125 ml (½ cup) flaked almonds, lightly toasted
20 ml (4 t) chopped preserved ginger
125 ml (½ cup) light sugar syrup (made in proportion 1 cup sugar : 3 cups water)
30 ml (2 T) freshly chopped mint leaves

In a chilled bowl, combine the cubed melon and sprinkle over the almonds. Stir the ginger into the syrup and drizzle onto the salad, tossing the fruit very gently. Sprinkle over the chopped mint and serve while still cold. Serves 2 or more. The recipe can be doubled.

Sefapane Lodge and Safaris

One minute we were driving down a busy road in the mining town of Phalaborwa. Seconds later, after turning into Sefapane's gateway, the scene was transformed into a lush, subtropical paradise, an unexpected 10 ha oasis of riverside greenery, lying between urban order and the Kruger National Park. Right on cue, an Openbilled Stork alighted on the branch of a leafless tree at the edge of the huge dam in front of us. His arrival served to corroborate the resort's claim to be a birder's paradise – and one where uncommon winged visitors like this can often be spotted.

The hard-to-find Openbilled Stork is a regular visitor

Restaurant manager Irene Shai welcomes diners with a smile

Offering an affordable alternative to Bushveld camps, Sefapane Lodge caters for travellers wanting a base for both day trips into the Kruger National Park and excursions to the numerous attractions of the Limpopo and Mpumalanga provinces.

This former caravan park has been transformed into a lush and tranquil retreat, where 30 fully serviced and air-conditioned rondavels cluster on stretches of lawn beneath indigenous trees. The gardens lead to a huge, reed-fringed dam that covers nearly a hectare. A notice en route warns visitors to 'Beware of the crocodiles'; another warns about the danger of hippos – in fact, both amphibians are rarely seen, although a resident monitor lizard has been known to alarm some overseas guests.

All the chalets are equipped with showers, fridges and sinks for self-catering, and there are a few family rondavels with three bedrooms.

Joris Bertens, who first encountered Sefapane as a visiting hotel school student from the Netherlands, returned in 1997, this time as proprietor, to convert and upgrade the property. He organises game drives and river safaris in the Kruger Park, followed by evening barbecues. The lodge supports a local African choir, and visitors can arrange to visit their village for a recital. Golfers will find the renowned Hans Merensky course just minutes away and Sefapane is hugely popular with birders, evidenced by the South African Birdlife logo at reception.

To beat summer temperatures of 40 degrees plus, Sefapane – which means Southern Cross – boasts a large swimming pool in a lush setting, adjoining a sunken bar and boma. The restaurant, which presents a menu of appetising, well-priced fare, is as popular with local residents as with visitors. We savoured a starter of smoked mountain trout, caught locally, followed by colourful and substantial salads.

Sefapane has entered the Bush Banquet Challenge every year since it began, taking home the Chaîne des Rotisseurs' trophy for service in 2005. The team was also placed in the Food and Wine Pairing and Service categories in the same year.

Sefapane advertises itself as offering 'Affordable African Experiences', a phrase which well sums up what's on offer at this tranquil resort.

OSTRICH LIVER PÂTÉ

Ostrich liver is quite strongly flavoured, so is diluted generously with butter, making this a rich pâté. Alternatively, use half ostrich, half chicken liver and reduce the butter by half. The recipe may also be halved.

1 kg butter
2–3 onions, chopped
1 kg ostrich liver, cleaned and roughly chopped
50 g thyme leaves, stripped from stalks
5 tots (150 ml) brandy
salt and ground black pepper

TO ACCOMPANY
toast rounds
cranberry sauce
sour cream
red pepper slivers (optional)
fresh herb sprigs

Heat 100 g of the butter in a large, deep pan, add the onion and sauté for a few minutes. Add the ostrich liver in batches, and stir over high heat for a few minutes. Stir in the thyme and the brandy, reduce the heat, and cook, stirring frequently, until the liver is just cooked through.

Cool a little, then transfer the pan mixture to a food processor, add the remaining butter, and process to a smooth pâté. Season to taste, then spoon into a bread tin lined with plastic wrap, cover and chill.

Turn out when required, slice and serve on a flat plate with toast rounds. Drizzle around some cranberry sauce, add a dollop of sour cream on the side, and garnish with red pepper slivers, if using, and herbs.

Serves about 12 as a starter

PAN-FRIED CAMEMBERT IN PHYLLO

This starter course has been around for decades, but is still a firm favourite with diners. Sefapane does not accompany the cheese parcels with the traditional sweet berry dressing or jelly, but a spoonful could be added to each serving if wanted.

1 round of firm but ripe Camembert
½ sheet phyllo pastry, defrosted
melted butter
oil for deep-frying

TO SERVE
mixed salad leaves
toasted sesame seed dressing
red pepper slivers

Cut the cheese into four quarters. Cut the pastry in half, brush one half with butter and place the other half on top; cut the double layer into four equal pieces. Place one cheese quarter onto each pastry quarter and gather the ends to make a parcel. Deep-fry the parcels in hot oil, and drain on paper towel.

To serve, arrange the salad leaves on each of two plates. Drizzle the leaves with a little dressing. Top the salad with two cheese parcels. Garnish with red pepper slivers.

Serves 2

DILL AND NUT-CRUSTED SALMON WITH LEMON DILL SAUCE

Pecan nuts add irresistible Lowveld flavour to this classic fish dish.

20 ml (4 t) finely chopped fresh dill
60 ml (4 T) fresh breadcrumbs
15 ml (1 T) crushed pecan nuts
250 g fresh salmon fillet
white of 1 egg
15 ml (1 T) olive oil
salt and ground black pepper

TO SERVE
jacket or mashed potatoes
lemon dill sauce
fresh dill sprigs
1 lemon wedge
peri-peri powder (optional)

Combine the dill, breadcrumbs and crushed nuts. Coat the salmon on both sides with the egg white, then top with the crumb mixture. Heat the olive oil, and pan-fry the fish carefully on both sides to brown lightly. Season with salt and pepper, then transfer to an ovenproof dish and bake at 180 °C for about 15 minutes until cooked through.

Serve with your choice of potato and a spoonful of lemon dill sauce. Garnish with dill sprigs and a lemon wedge dipped into peri-peri powder, if liked. Wine pairing: The citrus and fennel flavours emanating from KWV's bone-dry Reserve Sauvignon Blanc makes this the perfect team mate.

Serves 1

TANDA TULA SAFARI CAMP

Our arrival at Tanda Tula on a superb autumn morning was well timed: we hopped onto a safari vehicle for a short drive across a grassy plain, then headed down through thick bush to the banks of a dry riverbed. Here, under a canopy of century-old trees, rustic tables and a cold buffet awaited diners. But it was the aroma of mushrooms and sausage, sizzling bacon and tomato drifting from huge black pans over a range of fires that made our mouths water. This brunch was a delectable introduction to a lodge where highly rated cuisine and elegant accommodation add allure to the bush experience.

The bush breakfast chefs seldom have leftovers

Head chef David Mathabula, both superb cook and great raconteur

Along with its reputation for excellent food, Tanda Tula is renowned for its beautiful thatched tents and for a high standard of service. Located in the Timbavati Game Reserve, this camp accommodates a maximum of 20 guests in luxurious seclusion, while offering game viewing in vehicles that can traverse thousands of hectares.

From private wooden decks overlooking the river, one is drawn into the canvas-walled tents exhibiting safari-style elegance. Bathrooms with Victorian baths and outside showers back the tents. There is no humming air-conditioning or mini-bar, and only mosquito netting between you and the animals of the bush. The sounds of the night are not muffled here.

The programme of game drives, bush walks and relaxation is punctuated by memorable meals served in the boma or the bush, the dining area or on guests' private decks. With menus that could start with loin of springbok served with red figs and rosemary, followed by seared yellowfin tuna with ratatouille and rösti and a finale of a lime and ginger crème brûlée, it's easy to see why Tanda Tula was the overall joint winner of the 2004 Bush Banquet Challenge.

Both head chef David Madisi Mathabula and F&B manager Odette Schuld are enthusiastic professionals responsible for this appetising fare.

Chef Mathabula, who was born and raised on the Timbavati reserve, has had 25 years of experience in game lodges, working his way up from waiter to his present position and presiding over the lodge's winning entry in the Bush Banquet Challenge.

He also has a fascinating store of stories about how the area has changed over the decades, from cattle farm to private family camp to the present commercial operation.

Tanda Tula, in collaboration with the international conservation organisation, Save The Elephants, is currently involved in a long-term elephant research programme, and interested guests can not only visit the research station but become actively involved. The multi-faceted programme includes research – where elephants are monitored through radio tracking – along with education, grassroots conservation, and protection.

Guests will also find their game drives enhanced by rangers whose fields of knowledge extend beyond wildlife to environmental goals and local history.

ROULADE OF PANCAKES WITH TOMATO SAUCE

This delicious vegetarian starter is substantial enough to double as a luncheon dish. Start a day ahead.

PANCAKES
3 eggs, lightly beaten
200 ml milk
70 g flour
10 ml (2 t) olive oil
salt
oil for frying

FILLINGS
1 kg leeks, white part only, washed
butter for frying
1 kg fresh spinach, washed and coarse stalks removed
500 g ricotta cheese
pinch grated nutmeg
salt and pepper
1 kg pumpkin, peeled and cubed
±500 ml (2 cups) home-made tomato sauce
handful black olives, stoned (optional)

TO SERVE
butter
Parmesan cheese, grated
coriander sprigs

Make the pancakes: Combine the first four ingredients, whisk well and season with salt. Leave to stand for 1 hour, then heat a 30 cm diameter frying pan and cover the base with a thin film of oil. Make each pancake by cooking until both sides are browned. The batter will make 6 pancakes, which will be a little tougher than usual, as they will act as containers for the fillings.

For the fillings, chop the leeks, and fry in heated butter until tender. Cool, then purée the mixture and set aside. Blanch the spinach, dry well, then chop finely. Fry in heated butter until cooked. Remove from the heat, cool a little, then mix in the ricotta and season with nutmeg, salt and pepper.

Finally, place the cubed pumpkin on a baking tray, drizzle with a little oil and roast at 200 °C until tender. Cool, purée and season to taste.

To assemble, spread half the leek purée over one pancake, top with a second and spread with half the spinach mixture. Repeat with a third pancake, and spread with half the puréed pumpkin. Roll up the 3 pancakes and wrap in foil. Repeat the process with the 3 remaining pancakes and remaining fillings. Chill the rolls overnight.

When ready to serve, slice the roulades thickly. Dot each slice with butter, sprinkle with Parmesan and grill until golden brown and heated through. Stir the olives, if using, into the tomato sauce, and heat the sauce.

Serve the roulades on a pool of sauce and garnish with a coriander sprig.

Serves 6

HERB-CRUSTED RACK OF LAMB WITH RISOTTO AND RED WINE SAUCE

A splendid creation for a special dinner, which could be varied by using rosemary and thyme in the crust and replacing the risotto with crispy baked potato balls.

2 racks of lamb, each with 8 chops, skinned and chined
salt and black and cayenne pepper to taste

SPARKLING WINE RISOTTO
400 g risotto rice
1.5 litres chicken stock
200 g butter
50 ml (3 T plus 1 t) olive oil
1 medium onion, chopped
50 ml (3 T plus 1 t) sparkling wine
few saffron threads, soaked in a little stock
ground black pepper
shaved Parmesan cheese

AMARULA CREAM™ SAUCE
1 onion, chopped
butter
500 ml (2 cups) beef stock
250 ml (1 cup) dry red wine
Amarula Cream™ liqueur to taste
flour

HERB CRUST
30 ml (2 T) mustard powder
125 g softened butter
200 ml (⅘ cup) fresh breadcrumbs
200 ml (⅘ cup) finely chopped watercress
200 ml (⅘ cup) finely chopped parsley leaves
2 cloves garlic, crushed
30 ml (2 T) green peppercorns, crushed

Preheat the oven to 200 °C. Portion the lamb into five sections of 3 chops each, reserving the remaining chop for another use. Score the fat diagonally in both directions, making a lattice pattern. Season and place, fat side up, in a roasting pan and roast until the meat is just sealed, then remove and cool.

Make the risotto in the usual way, substituting 50 ml sparkling wine for the same quantity of chicken stock. Leave for 10 minutes before serving.

For the sauce, fry the onion in a little heated butter until golden. Stir in the stock, red wine and liqueur to taste and simmer for 15 minutes. Thicken the sauce with a beurre manié (an equal mixture of butter and flour).

Make the herb crust by mixing the ingredients to a paste. Pat this over the top of the racks of lamb and leave at room temperature. Return the meat to a preheated oven and roast for 30 minutes, then serve immediately, accompanied by the risotto and red wine sauce. Wine pairing: This brilliant lamb dish deserves the best: Pour KWV's Cathedral Cellar Cabernet Sauvignon or try the Cathedral Cellar Merlot.

Serves 4–5

KWV
ESTABLISHED 1918
2002
CATHEDRAL CELLAR
MERLOT
PRODUCED BY KWV PAARL SOUTH AFRICA

ROOIBOS 'CRÈME BRÛLÉE' WITH STRAWBERRIES

Here South Africa's indigenous bush tea and white chocolate combine to add distinctive flavours to this baked 'crème brûlée'.

1 litre (4 cups) cream
240 g castor sugar
1 vanilla pod
1 cinnamon stick
120 g white chocolate, broken into pieces
6 rooibos tea bags
12 egg yolks, whisked
fresh strawberries, hulled and sliced
seasonal fruit and mint to garnish (optional)

In a large saucepan, combine the cream, sugar, vanilla, cinnamon and chocolate, and heat to scalding point, stirring occasionally, until the chocolate has melted and the mixture is smooth. Remove from the heat and leave to cool. Steep the tea bags in the warm cream mixture. Preheat the oven to 150 °C.

When the cream mixture has cooled to room temperature, remove the vanilla pod, cinnamon stick and tea bags, and discard. Stir in the egg yolks, pass the mixture through a sieve, then divide evenly between 6–8 ramekins. Top each with sliced strawberries, arranged decoratively. Place the ramekins on a deep baking tray, add sufficient warm water to reach halfway up the sides of the ramekins and bake for about 1 hour or until set. Chill for about 3 hours, but serve at room temperature. Garnish with sliced fruit and mint leaves, if liked.

Serves 6–8

ICED COFFEE

Even coffee addicts prefer this version of their fix when Lowveld temperatures soar towards the 40 °C mark.

±50 ml (3 heaped T) pure instant coffee
±50 ml (3 heaped T) powdered drinking chocolate
sugar to taste
250 ml (1 cup) boiling water
500 ml (2 cups) cream
±1 litre (4 cups) milk
ice cubes

Place the coffee, chocolate and sugar in a large jug, pour in the boiling water and stir until the coffee and chocolate have dissolved. Stir in the cream, then whisk. Stir in the milk and chill.

To serve, pour the coffee over ice cubes.

Serves up to 6

Raptor's View Estate and Welverdiend Guest House

Strangler Fig and Tree Wistaria, Marula and Bush Willow, Fever Trees and Wild Olives ... In times of yore, farmers and their wives planted for shade, for beauty, for fruit and flowers. Their chosen species were not necessarily indigenous, but, several generations on, these mature trees present a magnificent display around the former farmstead on Welverdiend. Manager Michelle Venter welcomed us, adoring dogs in tow, and said that this former hunting farm now plays a happier role as a well-stocked game reserve. The 1 300 ha are accessible not only to guests, but to visitors and homeowners at neighbouring Raptor's View.

Testimony to drought and hungry herbivores

Welverdiend Guest House is a veritable oasis in the Bushveld, offering guests sweeping lawns (kept well trimmed by passing kudu and warthog), a treasury of magnificent trees, and tranquil gardens that lead from a deep veranda to a braai boma with endless views to a backdrop of the Drakensberg range.

Ideal for travellers wanting to base themselves near Hoedspruit and explore the area in a series of day trips, the guesthouse is managed by ardent animal-lover Michelle Venter, who doubles as unofficial nurse to a variety of injured animals.

The neighbouring property, another former farm, is Raptor's View, now a wildlife estate and the site of several exciting projects, one of which is the Southern Cross Schools. Their spacious buildings and grounds are sited within the 1 000 ha estate, fully fenced by electrified game fencing and patrolled 24 hours a day.

Raptor's Lodge consists of a complex of 20 well-designed and very sturdily built two-bedroom, two-bathroom thatched homes. While these make desirable retirement homes, they are also earmarked by city-dwellers for weekend and holiday use, giving owners not only an African bush experience, but membership of the nearby Drakensig Country Club, which offers sporting facilities and golf.

These sectional title units can also be pooled into a rental scheme that enables owners to get a return on their investment.

Raptor's View homes are designed for year-round alfresco dining.

A second option at Raptor's View is the purchase of 1 ha sites on the estate, where owners build homes on plots separated from neighbours by game tracks, woodland and waterholes. Lucky are the children growing up in these surroundings, where you may have to contend with a baby giraffe that has slipped while drinking and is now thrashing around in your swimming pool, but where family living and the African bush experience meld into an enviable lifestyle.

Everyone who lives or stays on Raptor's View Estate has automatic access to game drives through Welverdiend Game Reserve, where white rhino and leopard may be seen.

When the idea of self-catering palls, the hospitable staff at both the guesthouse and lodge will whip up a delectable picnic to be savoured in these tranquil yet wild surroundings.

BUSH BREAKFAST SMOOTHIES

While this makes the ideal breakfast-on-the-run, it's best sipped slowly, while watching the sun rise over the Bushveld.

1 ripe mango, peeled and diced
±¼ medium pawpaw, peeled and diced
250 ml (1 cup) natural, low-fat yoghurt
±5 ml (1 t) marula jelly or to taste
3–4 ice cubes or to taste

Combine all the ingredients and blend until smooth.
Serves 1

CHICKEN, BACON AND AVOCADO BAGUETTE

This is also known as the Bush Man's Stack Pack.

1 just-baked French loaf
butter or olive oil
handful of rocket leaves
2 firm, ripe avocados, halved, flesh sliced
fresh lemon juice
about 6 rashers streaky bacon, rind removed and grilled until crisp
handful lettuce leaves
3 grilled chicken breasts, boned and flesh broken into bite-sized pieces
handful jalapeno peppers, cut into strips (optional)
salt and ground black pepper

Slice the bread lengthwise and butter the insides or sprinkle with olive oil. Using one half as a base, build up the filling: start with the rocket, then add a layer of avocado, which has been sprinkled with lemon juice, and top with bacon. Cover this with lettuce leaves then arrange the chicken over them and finish with jalapeno peppers, if using. Season lightly with salt, generously with black pepper, drizzle over a little olive oil and top with the other bread half. Wrap in plastic wrap, weigh down with cans, if wanted, and keep chilled until ready to travel. Slice thickly before serving. Wine pairing: KWV's zesty Sauvignon Blanc will make a refreshing companion to this portable lunch.

Serves 2–4, depending on appetite

TORTILLA WITH SMOKED TROUT

There's renewed interest in Spanish cuisine, and this version of their famous omelette makes perfect picnic fare. It stars smoked trout from the Lowveld, but you could also use smoked salmon offcuts. Cooking the potatoes in the pan instead of pre-cooking them improves the final result.

450 g potatoes, peeled and diced
1 large or 2 medium onions, finely chopped
300–350 ml light olive oil
salt
about 200 g smoked trout, flaked into strips
freshly ground black pepper
150 g creamed cottage cheese or cream cheese
3 extra-large eggs, preferably free-range, whisked together
sprigs of oregano (optional)

Mix the potato and onion together. Heat nearly all the oil in a large frying pan, add the potato mixture and stir. Reduce the heat, season with a little salt and cook the vegetables, stirring gently but often, until the potato is cooked through. Using a slotted spoon, remove the vegetables to a bowl and gently fold through the trout. Grind over plenty of black pepper.

Pour out the oil and residue in the pan.

Whisk the cream cheese into the eggs, then stir the potato mixture into this.

Return the pan to medium heat, add a thin film of oil and heat for a few seconds before pouring in the egg mixture and spreading evenly. Cook for about 2 minutes, then place a large oiled plate over the pan and invert the omelette onto the plate. Return the pan to the heat, adding the last teaspoon of oil. Slide the omelette back into the pan and cook for 1 more minute. Turn out and garnish with oregano, if liked.

As picnic fare, this is best cut into squares and served at room temperature, with crusty bread on the side.

Serves 4 as an appetiser

EXOTIC PICNIC FRUIT SALAD

Several Lowveld subtropical fruits star in this summery salad. Other fruit such as banana or nectarine can replace some ingredients.

1 punnet fresh strawberries, halved if large
pulp from about 6 granadillas (passion fruit)
about 4 kiwi fruit, peeled and sliced
1 large ripe mango, peeled and diced
about 20 litchis, peeled and pips removed
60 g dried, stoned dates, chopped
125 ml (½ cup) balsamic vinegar
brown sugar to taste
juice of 2 oranges

TOPPING
1 tub smooth cottage cheese
about 100 ml fresh cream
30 ml (2 T) castor sugar
fresh mint leaves, roughly chopped, to garnish

Combine the fresh fruit with the dates, pour over half the balsamic vinegar, and gently toss to mix. Add a little brown sugar, then stir in the orange juice and mix gently. Cover and chill for 1 hour, then taste again and add more balsamic, if wanted. Whip the cottage cheese with the cream and castor sugar, and chill separately. Serve the fruit salad topped with a dollop of the cream mixture and garnish with mint.

Serves 4 or more

CAMP JABULANI

No matter how many times one is privileged to get up close and personal with elephants in the bush, the experience is both moving and memorable. Here anticipation reached new heights as we were taken to meet a very special team of jumbos who were to carry us on a two-hour safari that was a highlight of our visit. After this unique journey it seemed quite in keeping that we had to cross the riverbed on a high suspension bridge to reach our suites, a walk that also served to suspend reality in favour of a wilderness world of unlikely luxury.

Baby Jabulani with dedicated keeper Flippie Botha

Palatable fare, prettily plated, is a hallmark of chef Lezaan Stroh's cuisine

Wildlife enthusiasts across the globe followed the heart-rending story of Jabulani, the baby elephant orphan, a few years ago. Screened in three episodes on the popular South African television programme 50/50, viewers applauded the efforts of dedicated care-givers who enabled an abandoned, scared, three-month old cub to survive – then thrive – as he grew up among humans who dedicated their waking hours to his health and happiness.

When attempts to release Jabulani back into the wild were unsuccessful, he was introduced to a team of trained elephants rescued from Zimbabwe. Today this international celebrity, still too young to be ridden by guests, nevertheless heads the procession on daily bush walks through Kapama Private Game Reserve. He has also lent his name to this recently opened camp, a luxurious destination and one of several that operate in Kapama Private Game Reserve, 13 000 ha of Bushveld that is reached within minutes from the Eastgate airport near Hoedspruit.

For those with limited time, and for those who prefer conventional, hotel-style accommodation, Kapama Lodge offers spacious en suite rooms with double doors to private stoeps. The thatched reception area overlooks a large lake where birdlife proliferates in the reed-fringed waters.

Buffalo Camp provides another option, where eight stylish, tented suites, linked by wooden walkways, perch high above a riverbed.

Kapama also offers day visitors game drives followed by gourmet braais (barbecues).

At Jabulani, guests are pampered in 5-star comfort, from the reception area where elephants feature in the décor, to the opulent lodges with colonial-style living areas and fireplaces, exotic bathrooms and private decks sporting rimflow plunge pools.

Game drives and visits to the Hoedspruit Endangered Species Centre are part of the recommended programme, with the elephant-back safari a memorable highlight for most guests.

When it comes to mealtimes, visitors are spoiled for choice as Lezaan Stroh, the camp's dedicated and highly professional chef, presents sophisticated, prettily plated courses in an apparently effortless gourmet progression. Informal breakfasts, alfresco lunches and formal dinners make dining an integral part of the pleasure of being at Jabulani.

JABULANI'S BUTTERNUT AND ONION QUICHES

This stylish vegetarian starter can double as a main course for small appetites.

1 small butternut squash, peeled and cubed
sunflower or light olive oil
1–2 onions, thinly sliced
15 ml (1 T) oil
15 ml (1 T) butter
30 ml (2 T) treacle sugar
45 ml (3 T) balsamic vinegar
1 egg
50 ml milk
50 ml cream
30 ml (2 T) creamed or smooth cottage cheese
salt and pepper to taste
melted butter
1 packet phyllo pastry, defrosted if frozen

TOMATO BUTTER
2 firm, ripe tomatoes, skinned, seeded and diced
fresh chives, finely chopped
salt and ground white pepper
fresh lemon juice
60 ml (4 T) butter

Toss the butternut cubes in a little heated oil in a pan until they start to darken, then transfer to a preheated oven at 180 °C and bake for about 20 minutes until tender.

Meanwhile, caramelise the onions by heating the second measure of oil and butter together in a pan, then cook the onions until softened. Add the sugar and vinegar, and cook until the vinegar has evaporated. Set aside.

Make the custard by whisking together the egg, milk and cream, and stirring in the soft cheese. Season to taste.

To make the pastry cases, brush the insides of four muffin cups with melted butter. Cut the phyllo pastry into 13 cm squares, and brush each with melted butter. Place three sheets in each of the four muffin cups at varying angles, so that the corners form a star shape.

Divide the diced butternut between the pastry cases and top up each one with the custard filling. Bake at 180 °C for about 20 minutes, until the custard has set.

Meanwhile, combine the diced tomato and chives, and season with salt, pepper and lemon juice. Place in a clean pan with the butter, and heat gently until the sauce is hot.

To serve, place a quiche in the centre of a plate and drizzle the tomato butter around each one.

Makes 4

JABULANI'S TORTILLA-WRAPPED SMOKED TROUT SALAD

Angling for trout is popular in the Dullstroom area of Mpumalanga. Vary the filling ingredients as desired – creamed horseradish could add flavour and heat to the cottage cheese in the filling. Store-bought tortillas will make this even easier.

TORTILLAS
500 ml (2 cups) cake flour (250 g)
pinch of salt
50 g butter
125–180 ml water

FILLING
±3 smoked trout, filleted and flaked into large pieces
avocado pear, sliced and tossed in lemon juice
shredded lettuce
sliced tomato
salt and ground black pepper
smooth cottage cheese
cucumber ribbons to garnish

Mix the flour and salt together, then rub in the butter with your fingertips until the mixture resembles fine breadcrumbs. Gradually add sufficient water to form a soft dough. Knead for up to 10 minutes, until pliable, then cover and leave for 1 hour. Cut into 6 equal pieces and roll out thinly to make a tortilla. Cook each one in a non-stick pan over medium heat for a few minutes until it starts to crisp. Cover with a damp cloth until ready to fill.

Combine the first 5 ingredients of the filling, and season. Place about 2 T of cottage cheese on each tortilla, top with the filling and roll up tightly. To serve, cut the ends off the tortillas and slice at an angle through the middle. Garnish with cucumber ribbons made by slicing an English cucumber lengthwise using a vegetable peeler. KWV Laborie Sauvignon Blanc will partner this well.

Serves 6 as a starter or as part of a picnic buffet

JABULANI'S LOIN OF LAMB FILLED WITH HAM AND CHEESE

This would counter the chill of a winter's night game drive with protein-rich flavour.

4 x 250 g portions lamb loin, boned
4–6 pieces good baked ham or streaky bacon, finely chopped
1 clove garlic, crushed
30 g grated Parmesan cheese
mixed fresh herbs of choice, chopped
olive oil
4 large brown mushrooms, roasted

Cut a pocket in each of the lamb portions.

Combine the ham or bacon with the garlic, cheese and herbs, and moisten the stuffing with a little olive oil. Use this to fill the pockets in the meat, dividing evenly, and pin each pocket closed using toothpicks.

Carefully seal the filled lamb portions in hot oil on all sides, then transfer to a preheated oven and bake at 190 °C for 7–10 minutes, depending on the thickness of the meat.

Serve the lamb on a roasted mushroom with potato balls on the side, if desired. Chef Stroh adds a spoonful of garlic and rosemary jus made from lamb stock.

Serves 4

SPICED MANGO AND HONEY PARFAIT

Surrounding the game reserves are large farms where mango orchards can be seen, dripping with fruit from early summer until early autumn.

5 egg yolks
125 g castor sugar, or to taste
25 ml (5 t) honey
15 ml (1 T) ground mixed spice or equal quantities grated nutmeg, ground cinnamon and ginger
500 ml (2 cups) fresh cream
1–2 firm ripe mangoes, peeled and diced OR 1 x 410 g can mangoes in syrup, drained and diced

Whisk the yolks with the castor sugar until fluffy, then whisk in the honey and spices. Whisk the cream until stiff then fold into the egg mixture. Fold in the diced mango. Line a bread tin or individual moulds with plastic wrap, spoon the parfait into the prepared container/s and freeze overnight or until firm. Slice and garnish with mint or additional mango.

Serves 4–6

PHALABORWA COUNTRY MANOR

Selati Hospitality Training Academy

Our arrival at the school coincided with the end of exams. Having completed both theoretical papers and practicals, the students were close to exhaustion. It was not the best time to introduce the concept of this book and discuss their contributions. But no sooner had they heard the words 'Bushveld Banquet' than fatigue was forgotten and 18 students were transformed into animated, enthusiastic young chefs. A combination of talent, dedication and hard work resulted in their entries gaining places in several divisions of the 2005 Bush Banquet Challenge.

The future of our hospitality industry seems in good hands.

Demonstrating culinary skills at Selati

Selati students focus on theoretical aspects of gastronomy

While first-time visitors to Phalaborwa will encounter a hot, dusty mining town, the inhabitants have surrounded themselves with magnificent gardens, shady oases that also attract birdlife and small animals. The students at Selati are lucky to have a former mining club as their school and hostel: while they continue to use the restaurant and lapa for training functions, the administrative offices and guest suites now play a new educational role for up to 20 students. The buildings are set in grounds of nearly 5 ha, complete with a koppie (hill) with resident dassies and a large swimming pool, making it a home from home some are reluctant to leave.

Principal Coretha du Plessis is dedicated to the art of producing good food that is well presented and professionally served. She is passionate about imparting this knowledge to the next generation that will be managing game lodges and restaurants, and cooking in the kitchens of local resorts as well as international hotels. Most students enrol for the two-year diploma course, which is internationally recognised. After completion, some continue to the advanced diploma, with further optional study in London leading to a degree.

First-year students are trained in housekeeping, front office, bar and professional cookery, and practicals include catering, from a dinner for 10 to an event for 500 guests. During their second year they spend five weeks working at game lodges and local hotels, a week in the winelands of the Western Cape and some time at a local brewery. Visiting lecturers share their expertise on subjects like specialist baking, cheese, and Greek and Chinese cuisines.

It is a reflection of the high standard maintained at the academy that Coretha du Plessis has had to start a register of lodges and resorts wanting to employ successful graduates from Selati. Not only are potential students carefully scrutinised, but they have to work hard – cleaning en suite bedrooms is on the agenda during their first year!

The challenges posed by the Bush Banquet were tackled with enormous enthusiasm and, in spite their lack of experience and limited funds, they fielded teams in both the Silver and Gold categories of the 2005 event, and were awarded places in the Table, Service and Kitchen divisions. The menu for the next Banquet makes the subject for frequent debate.

BEEF OR VENISON FILLET STUFFED WITH KUDU LIVER AND BONE MARROW

Rich, but delicious winter fare from bush country, and a dish that won Selati recognition in the 2005 Bush Banquet Challenge.

300 g kudu liver, cleaned
150 ml milk
5 beef marrowbones
800 g kudu or beef fillet, cut into 4 x 200 g portions
10 ml (2 t) coriander seeds, toasted
salt and pepper

Cut the liver into 1 cm cubes and marinate in the milk for about 1–2 hours.
Bake the marrowbones in the oven until golden brown on both sides and the marrow is cooked though.
Remove the marrow from the bones and fry over medium heat with the marinated liver until the liver is done.
Grill the fillet to personal taste, and slice along the length to make a cavity for the stuffing.
Season with the coriander seeds, salt and pepper to taste.
Stuff the fillet with the liver and marrow mixture, and serve with roasted vegetables.
Serves 4

BANANA MASH

An unusual addition to puréed potato when accompanying curried dishes.

3 large potatoes, unpeeled
3 small bananas, unpeeled
50 ml (3 rounded T) cream
salt and ground black pepper

Place the potatoes in cold water, bring to the boil, reduce the heat and cook until tender. Cool, then skin and cut up. Grill the bananas over medium heat until the skin turns black. Cool, peel and mash the bananas. Add the cream to the potato, season to taste, then incorporate the mashed banana, mixing well. Serve with the curried chicken (see page 146).
Serves 4–6

BUTTERNUT AND BILTONG SALAD

African flavours dominate in this robust and versatile salad, here styled by enthusiastic students using shallot leaves as elaborate garnish.

2 small butternut squashes, peeled, seeded and cubed or sliced
1 bottle commercial Greek salad dressing
½ large red pepper, cored and chopped
400 g plain feta cheese, cubed
200 g good quality beef or game biltong, shaved into bite-sized pieces
salt and ground black pepper
snipped chives or other edible greenery for garnish

In a large saucepan, cook the butternut in the salad dressing until tender. Drain the squash, transfer it to a bowl and reserve the dressing in a separate bowl. Mix the red pepper and feta into the squash, return to the saucepan, and heat gently until the feta just starts to melt. Alternatively, keep the diced red pepper and arrange decoratively around the butternut. Transfer to a salad dish, mix in the biltong and season lightly. Drizzle over the reserved salad dressing, garnish with chives, herbs or edible greens, and serve warm or at room temperature.

Serves 4

CURRIED CHICKEN DRUMSTICKS FILLED WITH BACON

A student creation that may not be gourmet fare, but it makes an appetising, well-spiced dish that hungry holiday-makers will enjoy.

250 g lean bacon rashers, rinded and diced
12 chicken drumsticks
2 garlic cloves, chopped
2 cm piece fresh ginger, grated
1 green chilli, finely chopped
5 ml (1 t) ground cumin
5 ml (1 t) ground coriander
15 ml (1 T) chicken masala
5 ml (1 t) turmeric
45 ml (3 T) olive oil
1 large onion, chopped
2 pieces cassia
1–2 large ripe tomatoes, peeled, seeded and diced
salt and ground black pepper

Fry the diced bacon until cooked and crisp.

Either debone the drumsticks or cut a slit in each and loosen the skin sufficiently to make room for the bacon. Fill the cavities with cooked bacon, dividing equally, and secure the openings using toothpicks. Make a paste of the garlic, ginger and chilli. Mix the cumin, coriander, masala and turmeric together, then combine with the garlic mixture. Rub this paste onto the chicken and leave to marinate for about 30 minutes.

Heat the oil and sauté the onion until tender. Add the cassia and continue frying for 5 minutes.

Brown the drumsticks carefully by turning regularly, then stir in the tomato and sufficient water to make a sauce. Simmer the mixture until the chicken is tender and cooked through.

Season to taste. Serve 3 drumsticks per person with a choice of banana mash, rice or crusty bread to accompany.

Wine pairing: KWV's fruity, accessible Chardonnay will make a good partner to this.

Serves 4

Jackalberry Lodge

With impala and warthog blocking the path, we slowly made our way to Jackalberry Lodge, but in time to keep a breakfast date on a cool, cloudy morning. The weather well complemented the soothing effect this intimate, affordable camp exerted on our party. With hindsight, it seems a most appropriate place for Sue Godding to have dreamed up the idea of a unique school with an environmental code linked to the national curriculum. Sue, who was working here at the time, was joined by another young mother with similar dreams. In the shade of a Jackalberry tree the concept of Southern Cross Schools started taking shape.

Impala graze unconcernedly all around the lodge

Ready for action is head chef Margaret Mokwena

Situated in the Thornybush Private Game Reserve, this small lodge is notable for its friendly staff and a tranquil ambience that pervades both the public areas and the quietly elegant chalets. Offering excellent value for money, Jackalberry is also one of the few local places where children of all ages are welcome.

The setting of lounge, open-air dining area under thatch, and the bar and pool is superb, looking onto an endless stretch of Bushveld backed by the irregular outline of the Drakensberg mountains.

Jackalberry accommodates guests in three classic and one family chalet, a luxury suite and two bush chalets. They are all decorated with understated elegance, soft earthy colours and contrasting textures of sisal and wood, making them easy on the eye.

Mini-bars, safes, tea- and coffee-making facilities and air-conditioning are standard, while doors open onto decks that invite one to sit and gaze at passing wildlife, of which there is usually an abundance. These verandas face the home turf of a wide variety of animals: more than 60 species are found here, including lion, leopard, buffalo, rhino, elephant, hyena and cheetah, while more than 280 species of birdlife have been recorded.

Morning game drives are followed by brunch, evening drives are preceded by high tea and the evening ends with a three-course dinner. Mealtimes could be shared by a couple of tame yellow-billed hornbills, which will go as far as pecking on the windowpane to draw attention to those dining inside.

Head chef Margaret Mokwena presides over a kitchen team that presents buffets that are appetising and colourful while the table d'hôte dinners are as tempting. Breakfasts could start with a brilliant layered berry and yoghurt trifle, and dinner finish with a rich citrus-spiked crème brûlée. Both dishes are likely to linger in one's memory.

Chef Mokwena is a dab hand at meat cookery, while her assistant Khensani Cheriwa Khoto's special talent is cake-baking. They are also among the prime movers and shakers behind the winning entries that have seen Jackalberry awarded several places in the Bushveld Banquet Challenges of the last few years. In 2005 the lodge came first in the Service and Kitchen sections of the Silver Category, and shared the Chaîne des Rotisseurs' Trophy for best waitron with Sefapane.

MINNEOLA CRÈME BRÛLÉE

Minneolas are soft-skinned citrus fruits. Naartjies (tangerines) can also be used. The spun sugar cage adorning the dessert in the photograph adds class and crunch, but is an optional extra that requires skill and patience.

750 ml (3 cups) cream
1 vanilla pod
8 egg yolks
about 125 ml (½ cup) white sugar or to taste
1–2 minneolas, peeled and segmented
15 ml (3 t) white sugar, additional

Combine the cream and vanilla pod in a heavy-based saucepan and heat until the cream is close to boiling. Remove from the heat and leave to infuse for about 30 minutes, then remove the vanilla pod.

Whisk the eggs with the sugar until thick and pale, then pour in the cream, stirring continuously.

Return the cream and egg mixture to the saucepan and continue stirring over low heat until the mixture thickens a little, but does not boil.

Place 2 minneola segments each on the base of 6 ramekins and pour over the custard, dividing it equally.

Cover and chill until set.

About an hour before serving, sprinkle the additional sugar over the tops of the puddings, place the ramekins on a baking tray and flash under a preheated grill until the sugar caramelises.

Chill again until serving time.

Serves 6

Otters Den

Hoedspruit Endangered Species Centre

Bombyx Silk Mori

Khamai Reptile Park

Josmacs

White River Motor Museum

Alan McSmith Safaris

ATTRACTIONS AND ACTIVITIES

Whether your idea of fun-filled hours leans toward hurtling down a fast-flowing river in a tube, or exploring a village museum, examining creepy-crawlies or chilling at a bush pub, the Lowveld can oblige …

Watch wild dogs devour their lunch, admire vintage vehicles, take a chopper to the Berg or browse through private collections of African art.

Consider alternative means of transport, such as a mountain bike, microlight or hot air balloon.

Whatever your choice, there's a Lowveld entrepreneur ready to make sure you enjoy your pursuit, a few of which are featured on the following pages.

Spinning the silk at Bombyx Silk Mori

Keeping the silkworms well fed on mulberry leaves

BOMBYX SILK MORI

'Discover the secret of silk' is the invitation extended to visitors, and one would be hard put to find a more congenial place to do so than at this airy complex of thatched factory, gallery and restaurant.

Its location on the 24 Degrees South Country Estate off the R531 places the operation conveniently in the triangle bordered by roads to Tzaneen, Dullstroom, Phalaborwa, Hoedspruit, the Kruger Park's Orpen Gate and Nelspruit to the south. Travellers taking the Panorama Route or heading to the Kruger Park or the Canyon should schedule a stop here and enter the fascinating world of sericulture, with an oriental history stretching back some 5 000 years.

From 09:00 to 15:00 every day, a tour is conducted through the Silk Duvet Factory.

You will see those busy silkworms, ranging in size from minute to large and languid, chomping their way through countless mulberry leaves. Watch how the woman workers deftly process the silk cocoons into fillings for a range of snowy duvets and pillows, all handmade. These ultra-light covers and pillows not only make luxurious bedding, but are ideal for both cold and hot nights, repel mould and mildew, and are unattractive to insect invaders. For those suffering from allergies, asthma, sinus conditions and eczema, silk may offer relief as it is inhospitable to the house dust mite, and no chemicals are used in the manufacturing process.

While browsing through the Ivory Room and Gallery, revel in the feel of pure silk on your skin as you slip on a bathrobe, then dip into the samples of the SilkSa range. This range of locally created organic cosmetics contains real silk, blended with extracts from various indigenous plants. Silk is one of the purest proteins around, containing 18 amino acids, is also an anti-oxidant, and offers healing properties. Along with Silk Essence day and night creams, cleanser, toner and body creams, there are bath time treats and aromatherapy massage oils for sale.

Don't leave without a packet of Safari Bush-Pourri – instead of petals, you will take home the dried leaves of the Red Bushwillow, an indigenous deciduous tree, that have been scented with Marula essence. This purchase will benefit the Southern Cross Schools' Reach-A-Cross project. Finish your visit with a light meal or coffee and cake at the Cotton Club Café next door, which features elsewhere in this book.

BOMBYX SILK MORI
24 Degrees South Country Estate
Hoedspruit district
PO Box 691 Hoedspruit 1380
Tel: +27 (0)15 795 5564
Fax: +27 (0)15 795 5568
Cell: (0)72 467 3310

HOT AIR BALLOONING: LIGHTER-THAN-AIR FLIGHTS OVER THE LOWVELD

While it's possible to enjoy this magical experience in various beautiful parts of South Africa, here intrepid passengers have the added thrill of game spotting from the air as the huge balloon whispers over the reserves adjoining the Kruger National Park.

The operation is run by Dr Wynand Uys from Otters Den River Lodge. On the evening before the flight, after studying the wind direction forecast, a launching site is chosen that will place the balloon upwind of a good game spotting area. Passengers meet for coffee before sunrise as the eight-storey high balloon is inflated and prepared for flight. After a safety briefing, take-off is usually timed to watch the sunrise from the air. Then the pilot searches for a favourable wind that will allow the balloon to drift gently over the Lowveld landscape. Giraffe, wildebeest, zebra, warthog and a variety of antelope are nearly always seen, and rhino, buffalo, elephant and lion are quite often spotted.

Game spotting from a hot air balloon is a memorable experience

The flight lasts about an hour, and sparkling wine and fruit juice are served after landing, followed by breakfast at Otters Den River Lodge.

This operation uses two balloons, a Cameron 180 that carries the pilot and eight passengers, and a Head 120 that takes four passengers plus the pilot.

About 90 hot air balloons fly in South Africa, operated by about 40 pilots, all of whom belong to the Balloon and Airship Federation of SA, which is affiliated to the Aeroclub of SA. Balloon Air Services are licensed both by the Department of Transport and the Civil Aviation Authority, and are subject to 100-hour inspections, air worthiness certificates and 'release to service' certificates.

If weather conditions don't permit flying on the day of the booking, passengers may request a full refund or can carry their ticket over to another day.

Otters Den also offers white water rafting in the Blyde River Canyon and Olifants Gorge, and have trained more than 100 adventure guides and six trip leaders since they started operations.

Otters Den River Lodge is on an island in the Blyde River
Tel: +27 (0)15 795 5488
E-mail: info@ottersden.co.za
Website: www.ottersden.co.za

Wild Dog, cheetah and various cat species are bred at the Hoedspruit Centre. The vultures enjoy the leftovers after feeding times

HOEDSPRUIT ENDANGERED SPECIES CENTRE

Even if your itinerary is crowded, try to find time to spend an hour or two at this remarkable centre on Kapama Game Reserve, not far from Hoedspruit in Limpopo province. Established in 1990 as a breeding programme for the endangered cheetah, the project has broadened to include the breeding of the equally endangered Wild Dog and other less publicised species such as Black-footed Cat and the African Wild Cat.

Some of these programmes are being carried out in co-operation with the National Zoology Department of the University of Pretoria.

The veterinary staff run an animal hospital where injured and abandoned animals are cared for prior to being released back into the wild.

Some 75 cheetahs were in residence when we were there, many of which had been rescued. Some were ready to be released back into the wild while others will be kept for breeding.

While you can only view the cheetah a few metres from their fenced camp, you can climb onto an open Landrover and be driven into the Wild Dog camp. Try to get there at feeding time, as this makes a memorable experience.

A 9 ha camp is home to about 15 Wild Dogs. The breeding programme is enjoying a high success rate, and the dogs recently used the base of a prominent termite hill in the camp as a burrow for a litter of nine pups.

At feeding time, staff empty large bags of raw meat onto the ground, which is a signal for the dogs to converge to feast, amid much mock fighting and growling.

Equally ready for lunch were white-backed and hooded vultures, which gathered in the surrounding trees in ever-increasing numbers, until the branches sagged under their weight. As the dogs became sated, these scavengers swooped down on the leftovers, only to fly off again as a few dogs made half-hearted attempts to jump into the air and snap at them.

Tours depart hourly, last around two hours and start with a video presentation.

The Centre is a non-profit organisation, which is largely funded by means of entrance fees and the profits from the sale of items in the curio shop.

FOR MORE INFORMATION AND TO BOOK A TOUR:
Tel: +27 (0)15 793 1633 or (0)15 793 1825
Fax: +27 (0)15 793 1646
E-mail: info@cheetahresearch.org.za
Website: www.wildlifecentre.co.za

LEFT: Banana caramel pancake with cream
RIGHT: Leadwood statuettes

ART WITH PANCAKES

Few visitors to South Africa return home without having sampled one of Harrie's famous pancakes, either in Pretoria, Dullstroom, at Cape Town's popular Waterfront, or in the original Pancake House at Graskop, which has been operating for nearly 20 years.

This attractive little town is a popular base from which to explore the Escarpment and the Lowveld. The Graskop Hotel, backed by beautiful gardens, is a 3-star country inn that has been accommodating guests in hospitable style and with a fine table for decades.

Less renowned is the fact that the hotel, its adjoining gallery and Delagoa African Arts & Crafts shop, which fills the gap between hotel and restaurant, are all treasuries of African and contemporary art, collected by the avid art-loving owners Harrie Siertsema and Willem van Bergen over many years.

Stay in one of the 19 en suite bedrooms in the main hotel building and you will find that a South African artist, well known or up-and-coming, has decorated your room to his or her unique style, including examples of his or her work on the walls. Visit the ground floor gallery where exhibitions change every few months. Browse through the Delagoa collection which ranges from conventional craftwork to original objets d'art that are sourced from all corners of the vast African continent.

Then, satisfy the inner man at the Pancake House where further decisions revolve around which filling to choose from the dozens of delectable combinations. Photographer Richard van Ryneveld enthused endlessly over his tomato bredie pancake, a substantial meal in a wrap, while I can vouch for the indulgently scrumptious banana caramel filling, which comes with cream or ice cream as a finishing touch. Yum.

GRASKOP HOTEL
PO Box 33 Graskop 1270
Tel: +27 (0)13 767 1081
Fax: +27 (0)13 767 1348
E-mail: graskophotel@mweb.co.za
Website: www.graskophotel.co.za

HARRIE'S PANCAKES
Tel: +27 (0)13 767 1273
Fax: +27 (0)13 767 1349
Cor. Kerk and Louis Trichardt Streets, Graskop

DELAGOA AFRICAN ARTS & CRAFTS, GRASKOP
Tel: +27 (0)13 767 1081
Fax: +27 (0)13 767 1348

Donald Strydom heads a team dedicated to conservation, education and reptile research

KHAMAI REPTILE PARK

Even if the thought of snakes, spiders and scorpions is likely to make you shudder – in fact, *especially* if this is the case – don't miss out on a visit to this impressive educational and research station when planning your Limpopo itinerary. Although you may encounter several knowledgeable and dedicated staff members, try to meet founder and owner Donald Strydom. If you succeed, you will leave Khamai buoyed by a store of fascinating knowledge and impressed by this internationally renowned expert who is dedicated both to educating the public and protecting and conserving reptiles, arachnids, amphibians and bats.

Although the park, formerly known as Swadini, is open to the public, it does not rely on the passing trade for its existence. This probably accounts for the low-key décor at the gate – but don't be put off. Inside, visitors of all ages are taken to see crocodiles, snakes, leguaans (iguanas), scorpions, spiders, turtles and lizards. Children can be photographed with a large snake draped around their shoulders, if they wish, but the prime benefit of these visits is educational, and there is a shady tea garden for refreshments after the tour.

'Conservation through Education and Research' is the goal at Khamai, a short phrase that covers an extraordinary programme of activities undertaken by Donald and his team.

Veterinary students, both South African and international, use Khamai for research projects, while final year medical students from the University of the

Witwatersrand come to learn how to recognise and treat snakebites. Others who visit are nursing students, senior game rangers and trackers, and those who work for emergency services, including firemen. At Khamai they learn to identify, recognise, and deal with these animals rather than destroying them.

Education is taken to the public as well: Donald Strydom gives lectures to schools and clubs, conferences and professional groups at venues like game lodges and shopping centres, exhibitions and business schools.

Back at the park, he also offers de-sensitising courses for humans who are terrified of snakes or spiders, and claims a 100% success rate. Admiring some of his film clips on the big screen in the lecture hall, we learned about the documentaries he has made for television, while acting as scientific advisor to such prestigious organisations as the BBC and *National Geographic*.

Strydom and his staff know that their efforts are reaping results when they get calls for help. On the day we were there, a householder called to report finding a hole in his garden containing what looked like snake eggs, being guarded by some kind of reptile. Khamai staff responded and found that a cobra or black mamba had indeed laid the eggs, but the guardian was a tawny-plated lizard who had decided to share the shelter.

Khamai Reptile Park
12 km from Hoedspruit on the R527
PO Box 175 Hoedspruit 1380
Tel/Fax: +27 (0)15 795 5203
Cell: +27 (0)82 299 3981
E-mail: reptile@yebo.co.za

Join the locals at this riverside bush pub

JOSMACS BUSH PUB

This is the venue to head to to meet the locals – from rangers to townsfolk, farmers to chefs, managers to other hard-working people in the hospitality industry. It's where you can catch up with local news, meet friends, enjoy a sundowner and do a little game spotting on the side, for this laidback, rustic pub and restaurant enjoys a great location on the banks of the Klaserie River.

Whether you are propping up the bar or chilling at one of the rustic tables, you are likely to enjoy your drink while watching elephant, buffalo and antelope wandering through the tall reeds that line the riverbed below you.

Someone built a bat house on the edge of the bank, so that the sight of these little mammals swooping off on their nocturnal forays may enhance evening visits.

The restaurant serves conventional pub fare and there is affordable en suite accommodation in the small bed and breakfast establishment.

Josmacs Bush Pub
Argyle Road, after the Klaserie bridge
Hoedspruit district
Tel/Fax: +27 (0)15 793 2951

Both relaxing and adrenalin-charged activities are offered at the Blyde Canyon Adventure Centre

BLYDE CANYON ADVENTURE CENTRE

River rafting, microlighting, horseback riding, abseiling, tubing and kloofing – these are just some of the adventure sports that are offered by operators in the Lowveld. There are a few more relaxing options, like pleasure boat rides on the Blyde dam that families can enjoy together, but most of the options are adrenalin-charged, strenuous activities demanding varying levels of fitness.

Grade one to grade four rapids are negotiated during white water rafting trips down the Blyde River. The trip can be done in seven hours, or over two days with an overnight camp on the riverbanks. An easier option – and good introduction to the sport – is a full day's river rafting in the Olifants Gorge.

For adrenalin junkies there's little to beat abseiling down rocky outcrops, usually done in the area near the Strydom Tunnel. This is also where kloofing takes place, which involves climbing, jumping and walking through streams, followed by a little cave exploration.

Microlighting over the Canyon, the Olifants valley and nearby game reserves is exhilarating rather than strenuous – 20- and 30-minute flights are offered.

Even novice riders – and children from the age of five – can enjoy trips on horseback that will take them among game like giraffe, zebra and wildebeest. Game-viewing from quad bikes is another option.

CARL SMIT
Blyde Canyon Adventure Centre
Swadini Aventura resort
Hoedspruit district
PO Box 176 Hoedspruit 1380
Tel: +27 (0)15 795 5961
Cell: +27 (0)82 562 6379
E-mail: blydeadventure@lantic.net
Website: www.blydeadventure.com

FLIGHT OF THE DRAGON WITH MCFARLANE SAFARIS AND TOURS

There is something extra-special about boarding a chopper right at one's game lodge, taking off in a swirl of dust and dry leaves, then whirring through azure skies above the Bushveld. Far below passengers can spot the roofs of lodges and see trails through the bush, but soon the vistas change as the helicopter heads to the Escarpment. Here, where the Dragon Mountains (the Drakensberg) meet the Lowveld, passengers savour an aerial tour of the renowned Panorama Route. Pinnacle Rock, God's Window, Bourke's Luck Potholes and, of course, the Blyde River Canyon are as impressive from above as they are from earth, offering scenic evidence of their claim to being in one of the most beautiful regions in Africa.

After the chopper has descended to land at a shady spot in the Treur River gorge, summertime travellers may enjoy a swim in the cool mountain water before settling to a picnic lunch washed down with fine Cape wines.

This tour is taken in Bell Jetranger or Robinson 44 helicopters, and can be enjoyed by a minimum of two and a maximum of four travellers.

This is just one of many excursions and safaris visitors are offered by this efficient tour company. Take a journey to the Mountains of the Silver Mist; marvel at the giant Baobab tree; see the green hills of Limpopo cloaked in tea bushes; admire the Debegeni Falls; wonder at the hardships pioneers endured as they took the old wagon trail to the coast.

Golf enthusiasts can indulge in their passion, playing on the 18-hole championship course at the Hans Merensky Country Club situated in a game reserve.

Picnic in style after an exhilarating flight to the Drakensberg

While warthog frequent the fairways, giraffe and impala are regular spectators and the water hazards are home to hippo and crocodile. Clients can choose to get to their game of golf via chopper, small plane or by road.

Operating from an office in Hoedspruit, Garth and Viv McFarlane provide a reliable link between the Lowveld lodges and the myriad attractions of the region. They offer visitors a wide selection of classic day tours, longer safaris and extension tours that can include time in the Kruger National Park followed by trips to destinations in Mozambique. Their vehicles can be seen all over the Lowveld, transferring visitors from airports to lodges in the reserves and hotels in the towns. McFarlane safaris and tours are conducted in luxury air-conditioned mini-buses, led by experienced, knowledgeable, registered rangers and guides.

MCFARLANE SAFARIS AND TOURS
PO Box 983 Hoedspruit 1380
Tel: +27 (0)15 793 3000
Fax: +27 (0)15 793 3001
E-mail: info@mcfarlanesafaris.co.za
Website: www.mcfarlanesafaris.co.za

The Three Rondavels are one of the Blyde River Canyon's best viewpoints

THE PANORAMA ROUTE: A DRAMATIC, ROMANTIC, HISTORIC AND BREATH-TAKINGLY BEAUTIFUL CIRCUIT OF THE LOWVELD

The scenic highlights include spectacular gorges, sparkling waterfalls, stretches of savanna, picturesque villages and panoramas that unfold from a series of lookout points.

If you read older books on the area, the original Panorama Route seems to have been limited to the circular route between Pilgrim's Rest, Graskop and the loop that takes one to God's Window and the Pinnacle. Today the circuit has extended to incorporate a much larger area, taking in a sweep of the Lowveld that could be done in a few hours, but needs several days to do justice to its many attractions.

Collect a map from any tourism bureau in the region. It will cover the entire area from Hoedspruit in the north to Sabie and Hazyview in the south.

Taking Hoedspruit, one of the gateways to the Lowveld, as a point of departure, the R527 leads travellers through the Strydom Tunnel and the Abel Erasmus Pass. Turning east, the R532 heads straight into the Blyde River Canyon Nature Reserve, where the canyon, the third largest in the world, stretches south for nearly 30 km.

One of the finest viewpoints is from the Three Rondavels, rock formations which resemble the round African thatched huts of the same name.

Some 14 km further, Bourke's Luck Potholes is a must-see site. Named after an early gold prospector, a series of deep natural potholes, filled with green water, can be seen from viewing bridges. Along with a visitors' centre, there is a marked three-hour trail to the bottom of the canyon and this point is also the start of longer hiking trails.

Travelling south, visitors can pause at numerous waterfalls, including the Lisbon Falls, which are the highest in the area at a point where the Blyde River splits into three. Other major waterfalls that will be marked on the map are the Berlin Falls and the twin 56 m-high MacMac Falls, named after the old mining camp.

God's Window presents magnificent views of both the Canyon and the Lowveld stretching to the Kruger National Park in the west. There are several easy walking trails leading to various lookout points over the 300-m drop into the ravine.

Graskop is well situated for a meal or an overnight stay at this point, with Pilgrim's Rest a short drive away. This historic little town is well described as a living museum, although hawkers and beggars at the roadside can sometimes overwhelm visitors. A weekday stop is suggested, so that the well-preserved buildings and various museums can be explored in leisurely fashion – these should not be missed.

Back on the R532 the route continues south to Sabie, the rural centre of the timber industry. Here travellers have two options: taking the R536 to Hazyview and the Kruger National Park, or continuing south, then taking the R37 through the historic Long Tom Pass and continuing to Lydenburg.

Visitors leaving the Kruger National Park could plan to do the route in reverse, starting at Hazyview.

For information on the Panorama Route visit any tourism office in the region and pick up a map of the area.

Both traditional and contemporary fare star on Shangana's menu

SHANGANA CULTURAL VILLAGE
A TASTE OF THE SHANGAAN CULTURAL HERITAGE

From the minute that visitors step into the thatched reception area, where a board welcomes you with the message 'Hoyo Hoyo', guests are transported to a less familiar world, that of the Shangaan people.

This authentic venue is sited midway between the Kruger National Park and the Blyde River Canyon, where Shangaan villages are dotted around stretches of grassland and forested areas. Built by the local community, this village is shaded by ancient trees and is inhabited by descendants of Chief Soshangana.

This award-winning tourist project, started six years ago, offers an insight into the traditions, art, music and cuisine of the Shangaans.

Options include browsing through arts and crafts on sale in the Marula Market; a guided walking tour around the village, including a consultation with a sangoma; a traditional lunch or a full evening's entertainment in the royal kraal.

The village also houses a community training school, where 25 local school children are learning to apply contemporary design to traditional materials like fabric, beads, grass, pottery and carvings. Their work is also on sale at the market.

Those who choose the midday meal will find both traditional and contemporary fare on the menu. If mopani worms do not appeal, there are less exotic alternatives, from maize bread and baked pumpkin to sweet potato, mieliepap or samp with grated peanuts and marog (stewed wild greens). Diners could play it safe with conventional choices like chicken baked with wild thyme, or oxtail, or sample crocodile meat or impala.

Those booking for the evening festival will be taken into a dramatic fire-lit circle, ringed by huts, where the chief and his family gather to relive their history.

Choristers and dancers present the story of the Shangaan tribe as a spectacular musical. Refreshment comprises traditional beer and exotic snacks are offered from wooden trays. The wives of the chiefs serve the rest of the meal inside their huts. Few are likely to forget the stirring story of how King Shaka of the Zulus sent Soshangana to conquer the Tsonga in present-day Mozambique.

For all these events, it would be a good idea to phone ahead, and for those travelling in groups, booking is essential.

The entrance to the Shangana Cultural Village is on the R535 – 4 km outside Hazyview on the road to Graskop
Tel: +27 (0)13 737 7000
Fax: +27 (0)13 737 7007
E-mail: reservations@shangana.co.za or chief@shangana.co.za
Website: www.shangana.co.za

Take a tour through motoring history at Casterbridge

WHITE RIVER MOTOR MUSEUM

This museum is an intriguing and unexpected find, occupying some 2 000 m^2 of floor space spread over three levels. You will find it at the rear of an attractive country shopping complex on the outskirts of the Lowveld town of White River.

As owners Louis and Hans van der Merwe's personal collection of vintage vehicles was expanding swiftly, and the shopping centre presented an ideal site, the Motor Museum came into being. Soon their venerable vehicles were joined by others belonging to residents of the Lowveld.

Today there is an impressive display of more than 60 old-time cars, trucks and pickups, some restored, others still being lovingly tended by expert resident technicians Fred Bitter and Jan Plekker.

The oldest cars date back to 1911, and include a Swift, a Willys Overland and a Model T Ford.

Fast forward to 1924 and admire an eight-seater Packard Phaeton, formerly the property of Lord Delamere and found on his Kenyan estate in the 1970s.

One of the best-selling cars of all time, the Austin Seven, is represented in the museum by a 1929 model alongside another famous marque, an MG M-T from the same year. Among the trucks and pickups that have survived their working days are a 1926 Chevrolet and 1934 Ford AA.

The curators are very proud of the 1936 Jaguar SS100, the only one in South Africa, and one of only 314 to have been built.

Models of well-known makes from most of the subsequent decades of the 20th century can be found here, along with some interesting racing cars.

Give yourself more time than you think you will need at this museum: you will be glad that you did.

Casterbridge Farm Shopping Centre is also home to good restaurants and art galleries, as well as some inviting shops that range from designer fashion and jewellery to décor and gourmet outlets. Built on the site of a former mango plantation, the buildings occupy various levels between courtyards and gardens where original trees have been preserved.

There is also a cinema that screens art circuit movies and, nestled among old mango trees, the Barnyard Theatre for live music and entertainment.

Entrance to the museum is free.

The White River Motor Museum is open from 09:00 to 16:30 Monday to Saturday and from 10:00 to 15:30 on Sunday
Tel: +27 (0)13 750 2196
Website: www.motormuseums.co.za
Casterbridge Farm Shopping Centre
Corner of the R40 and Numbi roads
Tel: +27 (0)13 750 2196
E-mail: info@casterbridge.co.za
Website: www.casterbridge.co.za

Safari lunch in the making: smoking bream in the Okavango

ALAN MCSMITH SAFARIS

Here's a man who is truly passionate about the wilderness and who lives to share his passion with others. Alan McSmith achieves this by offering exclusive safaris and wildlife encounters that centre mostly, although not exclusively, around walking trails.

During his excursions through game reserves Alan has noticed how some clients, on coming into close contact with the wilderness, react with a sense of belonging while others gain spiritual direction after experiencing solitude in nature.

As a conservationist, he feels strongly that wilderness areas should not be developed merely to satisfy commercial ambitions.

A stylish safari picnic in a bush setting

Alan's camp in the Klaserie Game Reserve is a classic example of an African fly-camp. Made of canvas and reed, it caters for a maximum of six guests in three tents. Along with the kitchen and open-air hot bucket showers, there is a tented lounge and delicious bush cuisine is prepared over an open fire. While not luxurious, clients can expect a high standard of safari-style comfort and top-quality professional guiding.

Alan has guided professionally for 17 years, having led excursions through most of the major wildlife regions in southern Africa. As a self-proclaimed safari addict with an empathy for elephant, he has become known as one of the Lowveld's most experienced guides who can be counted on to maintain high standards.

Guests booking for his wilderness journey will embark on a five-day excursion through the Klaserie and Timbavati reserves. The programme is flexible, includes walking trails, game and night drives, and is planned according to game movement. The travellers will spend time among elephant herds, gain insight into the lives of nocturnal animals, learn how to track big game on foot and how to locate water in inhospitable terrain.

Alan McSmith also leads special safaris through Zimbabwe, Zambia and Botswana, where adventures centre on the Okavango Delta. Options include a 14-day traverse, a six-day exploration of the Okavango by powerboat and dugout canoe, and a six-day fly-fishing safari.

Sarah McSmith is a typical bush man's wife, providing logistical backup to Alan's safaris while keeping the home fires burning and the e-mails humming. She is also a dab hand at whipping up mouth-watering safari fare, combining improvisation and talent, a sure recipe for inspiring results. For a culinary experience with a difference, Sarah will whisk guests off to the bush where, while absorbing the wilderness experience, they can help prepare a meal that could include digging a hole to act as an oven, or cooking tortillas on a spade over the campfire.

ALAN AND SARAH MCSMITH
PO Box 1550 Hoedspruit 1380
Cell: +27 (0)83 472 4783
E-mail: safari@wintrails.co.za
Website: www.wintrails.co.za

As no book on Bushveld cuisine would be complete without a recipe for bread baked in a termite mound, here follows Sarah McSmith's recipe for Flower Pot Bread in a Termite Mound.

FLOWER POT BREAD IN A TERMITE MOUND

Along with the ingredients you will need the following equipment: one unoccupied termite mound; 1 medium clay flower pot; a small grid, preferably on legs, to hold the pot above the coals.

500 g bread flour
½ packet instant fast-acting yeast
large pinch salt
lukewarm water
additional 100 g bread flour

TOPPING
olive oil
sun-dried tomato in oil, drained
shaved Parmesan cheese

Soak the clay pot in water for about 15 minutes. Drain and line the inside with foil.

Place the first measure of flour in a large bowl, sprinkle over the yeast and salt, and mix well. Add sufficient warm water to make a sticky dough. Add the remaining flour, bit by bit, and knead to a soft, pliable dough. Cover with a towel and leave the bowl in a warm place for the dough to rise.

When it has risen to twice its size, knock it down and knead it again. Flatten the dough into a rough rectangle (the width should be half the height of the clay pot). Drizzle over a little olive oil, then scatter over pieces of sun-dried tomato and shaved Parmesan. Roll the dough up from the short end and place it into the clay pot. Set it aside to rise again.

Meanwhile, place about 3 shovelfuls of hot coals into the hollowed-out termite mound and spread out evenly. Place the grid in the centre of the coals, then place the pot on top. Close the termite mound entrance with a rock. Leave the bread to bake, checking after 15 minutes. It should take about 30 minutes, and is done when it sounds hollow when tapped.

THE 'CHAÎNE' CONTRIBUTION

SUPPORT FROM THE HIGHEST GASTRONOMIC LEVEL

It seems most appropriate that, since its inception in 2002, the Bush Banquet has enjoyed support from a venerable gastronomic association that originated as a 13th century guild of French goose roasters.

Limited as they were to cooking their birds on spits over mediaeval fires, these craftsmen founded a brotherhood that has developed into one of the most prestigious gastronomic associations in the world. La Chaîne des Rôtisseurs has more than 30 000 active members in 123 countries around the globe.

Similarly, the chefs from the game lodges, restaurants and hotels who compete in the annual Bush Banquet Challenge at Southern Cross Schools, produce magnificent three-course meals from their tented kitchens, despite the limitations of locality and those imposed by the rules of the contest.

Although the guild was disbanded, together with all others, during the French Revolution, it was revived by a group of French gastronomes in 1950. Today La Chaîne des Rôtisseurs has more than 30 000 active members in 123 countries around the globe.

The organisation is grouped into five regions or *Bailliages* in South Africa. The Pretoria *Bailliage* stretches from Pretoria in Gauteng into the Limpopo, North West and Mpumalanga provinces.

The Chaîne's history in South Africa dates back to 1981 when the first *Bailliage* was inaugurated in Johannesburg. Cape Town and Durban soon followed, while the Northern Transvaal, now called Pretoria, chapter was established in 1985. The Outeniqua *Bailliage* came into being at the start of the new millennium.

When the first Bush Banquet was held in 2002, word of the event reached the head of the South African 'Chaîne', as it is locally known. Allison Rutowitz – her official title being the Bailli Délégué du Bailliage d'Afrique du Sud – was delighted that chefs and their teams, who daily face the challenges of presenting quality meals to demanding international clientele from kitchens that are far from their suppliers, were to be recognised for their efforts. In addition, they were entering a cookout contest to raise funds for worthy causes.

The 'Chaîne' decided to endorse this culinary adventure, both to show their support and to indicate that dining well is not limited to meals served in fine dining venues. A sunrise breakfast and dinner under the stars can also be memorable, starring food, wine and top-quality service.

The committee also decided to recognise and motivate the local waiters taking part in the Bush Banquet through the annual presentation of a winner's

TOP LEFT: Chaîne VIPs Marie Jones, Hennale Steyn and Allison Rutowitz
TOP RIGHT: First winner of the Chaîne's service award, Andrew Nyathi of Royal Malewane

plate from the Chaîne. Their members monitor the service throughout the evening of the banquet, noting how contestants present courses and replenish guests' wine, and their depth of knowledge about the meal they are serving. The prize plates become the proud possessions of recipients, and this category has become a prestigious part of the Bush Banquet Challenge.

La Chaîne des Rôtisseurs is dedicated to the art of fine cooking, and to developing and promoting gastronomic values worldwide. The Bush Banquet, which also serves to raise culinary standards in the region, benefits from its association with this august body and the organisers are most grateful for their continued support.

Restaurants in South Africa that are professional members of the Association and consistently serve memorable meals may be awarded the Chaîne blazon, their highest international award. The Chaîne is also host to an annual Jeune Commis Rôtisseurs competition, an international contest limited to chefs under the age of 27.

For more information, log on to the local website at www.chaine.co.za and the international one at www.chaine-des-rotisseurs.net.

THE CAPE CONNECTION

KWV
ESTABLISHED 1918

FINE CAPE WINES AND MUCH, MUCH MORE

Starting in 2003 KWV International supported the Bush Banquets for three years, both by supplying wine from the Laborie range to complement the contestants' feasts, as well as injecting welcome financial support.

The Food and Wine pairing section of the Lowveld contest helps to educate staff in the hospitality industry in the art of matching wine to dishes on the menu.

The KWV involvement also served to connect the Lowveld and the Western Cape in agreeable ways: both regions are popular tourist destinations, and travellers' itineraries reflect this. While rivalry exists, each acknowledges the unique attractions of the other. Many a glass of fine KWV wine is raised in toasts to successful seasons in both areas.

In 2004 it was reported that KWV International sold more than two million cases of bottled wine, most of it to the overseas market. This giant production company has come a long way since it was founded as a co-operative in Paarl in 1918. No visit to the Cape winelands is complete without a tour of the huge cathedral-like cellars and a tasting of the wide range of quality wines produced here.

Early in the 20th century wine farmers in the Paarl area met to found the Koöperatieve Wijnbouwers Vereniging van Zuid Afrika Beperkt – to give it its full title – largely to address concerns about over-production. The new organisation aimed to stabilise the industry, dispose of surplus produce, and control and regulate the market.

This it continued to do for most of the century: in 1924 the co-op was empowered to fix the annual minimum price to be paid to farmers for their distilling of wine. In 1940 this control was extended to table wine, and no person could produce wine without a permit from KWV. In 1957 a scheme of quotas was introduced, and it was only in 1992 that the system was relaxed as the industry moved towards a free market system.

Although there were complaints about the tight hold the organisation exerted on the wine industry, their involvement also helped South African brandy to reach the high quality for which it is renowned.

In 1995 KWV International was founded to handle KWV's marketing in the international arena. Ten years later the company has positioned itself as a market leader, operating worldwide in more than 35 markets from its Paarl headquarters. KWV became a private company in 1997, its former members becoming shareholders, while administrative and regulatory functions became the responsibility of the Wine Industry Trust. The company focuses on building brands and developing its global distribution network. Investments in state-of-the art technical and production facilities have seen new red wine and white wine cellars established.

In 1999 KWV International released its icon label – Perold – a single vineyard shiraz at US$100, the highest priced wine in South Africa.

In 2004 new chairman Danie de Wet helped to pioneer the biggest BEE (Black Empowerment) deal in the country's agricultural sector, as just over 25% of ownership was transferred to Phetogo.

KWV products were launched into the local market in 2003, with new marketing strategies being unveiled in 2005.

The company's top range, Cathedral Cellar, is rated highly by connoisseurs across the globe, while both the KWV Reserve and Classic wines are renowned for consistent quality. Laborie is another popular range owned by KWV. Wines from these ranges were used to suggest pairings with the main course recipes in this book.

Gracious KWV headquarters in Paarl

LIMPOPO
MPUMALANGA
Kruger National Park
DRAKENSBERG
Lulekani
Murchison
Gravelotte
Namakgale
Phalaborwa Gate
Sefapane
Selati Academy
Phalaborwa
Masorini Museum and Picnic Site
Letaba
Massingir Dam
Olifants
Balule
Selati Game Reserve
Ga-Selati
Garonga
Greater Makalali Game Reserve
Karongwi GR
Makhutswi
Kuname
Mica
Olifants
Balule Game Reserve
Klaserie Private Reserve
Blyde Olifants Conservancy
Motswari
Nhlaralumi
Tanda Tula
Umlani
Timbavati Private Nature Reserve
Akeru
Roodewal
Timbavati Picnic Site
Satara
N'wanetsi
Diphuti
Raptor's View
Hoedspruit
Eastgate
Camp Jabulani
Thornybush GR
Royal Malewane
Jackalberry
Cotton Club Café
Kapama GR
J.G. Strijdom Tunnel
Abel Erasmus Pass
Echo Caves
Blydepoort Dam
Klaserie
Orpen
Orpen Gate
Museum
Picnic Site
Timbavati
Sweni
Andover GR
Manyeleti Game Reserve
Acornhoek
Cottondale
Blyde River Canyon NR
Bourke's Luck Potholes
Vaalhoek
Ohrigstad
Voortrekker Graves
Old Voortrekker Road
Baobab Tree
Trichardt Memorial
Ngwenyeni Dam
Tintswalo
Vuyatelo in Djuma
Sabi Sand Game Reserve
Tshokwane Picnic Site
Orpen Plaque
Memorial Tablets
Blyde
Robbers Pass
Bushbuckridge
God's Window
Pilgrims Rest
Graskop
Ohrigstad Dam
Ohrigstad Dam NR
Mount Sheba NR
Kowyn Pass
Mac-Mac Falls
Marite
Mkhuhlu
Paul Kruger Gate
Lion Sands
Skukuza
Hazyview
Phabeni Gate
Rissington Inn
Gustav Klingbiel NR
Sabie
Horseshoe Falls
Lydenburg
Kiepersol
Sabie
Nhlotini
Sunset Dam
Sterkspruit NR
Long Tom Pass
Hendriksdal
Numbi Gate
Pretoriuskop
Buffelskloof NR
Sudwala Caves
Brondal
White River
Plaston
Renoster Pan
Picnic Site
Biyamiti
Crocodile Bridge
KRUGER MPUMALANGA INTERNATIONAL AIRPORT
Pienaar
Mthethomusha Game Reserve
Berg-en-Dal
Hectorspruit
Komatipoort
Crocodile
Schoemanskloof
Montrose
Montrose Pass
Montrose Falls
Nelspruit
KaNyamazane
Malelane
Karino
Kaapmuiden
Lebombo

KEY

- *National route*
- *Main route*
- *Minor route* — tarred / untarred
- *Scenic route*
- *Distance in km* — 10
- *Route numbers* — N4 40
- *River and dam*
- *Waterfall*
- *Border crossing*
- *Kruger Park gate*
- *Kruger Park camp*
- *Private camp lodge*
- *National airport*
- *Airfields* — main / minor
- *Place of interest*
- *International border*
- *Provincial border*
- *Private Reserve*
- *Kruger Park*

RECIPE INDEX

Page numbers in **bold** indicate photographs.

DESTINATION DIRECTORY

Akeru Safari Lodge
Timbavati Game Reserve
PO Box 69 Kiepersol Mpumalanga 1241
Tel/Fax: +27 (0)15 793 2250
E-mail: akeru@soft.co.za
Website: www.akeru.co.za
Reservations Tel/Fax: +27 (0)13 751 1374

Camp Jabulani
Kapama Private Reserve
Tel: +27 (0)15 793 1265
Fax: +27 (0)15 793 1261
E-mail: res@kapama.co.za
Website: www.kapama.co.za
Central reservations – PO Box 912031
Silverton 0127

The Cotton Club Café
Bombyx Mori Silk
Hoedspruit district
Tel: +27 (0)15 795 5564
Fax: +27 (0)15 795 5568
Cell: +27 (0)72 467 3310
E-mail: sue@bombyx.co.za

Garonga Safari Camp
Tel: +27 (0)82 440 3522
E-mail: reservations@garonga.com
Website: www.garonga.com
Reservations TSA Marketing
PO Box 2058 Parklands 2121
Tel: +27 (0)11 537 4620/25
Fax: +27 (0)11 447 0993

Jackalberry Lodge
PO Box 1055 Hoedspruit 1380
Tel: +27 (0)15 793 2980
Fax: +27 (0)15 793 2750
E-mail:
reservations@jackalberrylodge.co.za
Website: www.jackalberrylodge.co.za
Reservations – Gametrackers
Management SA (Pty) Ltd
PO Box 781549 Sandton 2146
Tel: +27 (0)11 463 3551/Fax: 463 2037

Kuname River Lodge
PO Box 15 Tzaneen 0850
Tel: +27 (0)15 383 0058
Fax: +27 (0)15 383 0056
Cell: +27 (0)82 330 3995
E-mail: lodge@kuname.co.za
Website: www.kuname.co.za

LION SANDS PRIVATE GAME RESERVE
River Lodge and Ivory Lodge, Sabi Sand Game Reserve, Mpumalanga
PO Box 30 White River 1240
Tel/Fax: +27 (0)13 735 5000/5330
E-mail: res@lionsands.com
Website: www.lionsands.com
Marketing: PO Box 2667
Houghton 2041
Tel/Fax: +27 (0)11 484 9911/9916

MOTSWARI GAME RESERVE
PO Box 67865 Bryanston 2021
Tel: +27 (0)11 463 1990
Fax: +27 (0)11 463 1992
E-mail: reservations@motswari.co.za
Website: www.motswari.co.za

RAPTOR'S VIEW WILDLIFE ESTATE & WELVERDIEND GUEST HOUSE
Raptor's View Sales Office, Hoedspruit
Tel: +27 (0)15 793 0471/3
Fax: +27 (0)15 793 0472
E-mail: annie@jordanprops.co.za
Jordan Properties Sales and Marketing
PO Box 782738 Sandton 2146
Tel: +27 (0)11 803 3777
Fax: +27 (0)11 803 7046
E-mail: info@jordanprops.co.za
Website: www.jordanprops.co.za

RISSINGTON INN
PO Box 650 Hazyview 1242
Tel: +27 (0)13 737 7700
Fax: +27 (0)13 737 7112
Cell: +27 (0)82 327 6842
E-mail: info@rissington.co.za
Website: www.rissington.co.za

ROYAL MALEWANE
PO Box 1542 Hoedspruit 1380
Tel: +27 (0)15 793 0150
Fax: +27 (0)15 793 2879
E-mail: info@royalmalewane.com
Website: www.royalmalewane.com

SEFAPANE LODGE & SAFARIS
PO Box 1621 Phalaborwa 1390
Tel: +27 (0)15 780 6700
Fax: 2+7 (0)15 780 6711
E-mail: reservations@sefapane.co.za
Website: www.sefapane.co.za

SELATI HOSPITALITY TRAINING ACADEMY
PO Box 255 Phalaborwa 1390
Tel: +27 (0)15 781 1128
Fax: +27 (0)15 781 1628
Principal Coretha du Plessis
Cell: +27 (0)84 513 3396
E-mail: selatiha@mailbox.co.za and coretha@mailbox.co.za

TANDA TULA SAFARI CAMP
Tel: +27 (0)21 794 6500
Fax: +27 (0)21 794 7605
E-mail: tandatula@uitsig.co.za
Website: www.tandatula.co.za
Reservations: reservations@uitsig.co.za

TINTSWALO SAFARI LODGE
PO Box 309 Hoedspruit 1380
Tel: +27 (0)15 793 0419 or 793 9013
Fax: +27 (0)15 793 0406
E-mail: info@tintswalo.co.za
Website: www.tintswalo.com
Reservations Tel/Fax: +27 (0)15 793 2513

UMLANI BUSH CAMP
PO Box 11604 Maroelana 0161
Tel: +27 (0)12 346 4028
Fax: +27 (0)12 346 4023
E-mail: info@umlani.co.za
Website: www.umlani.com

VUYATELA IN THE DJUMA GAME RESERVE
PO Box 338 Hluvukani 1363
Vuyatela: Tel: +27 (0)13 735 5555
Bush Lodge Tel: +27 (0)13 735 5366
Galago: Call reservations
E-mail: djuma@djuma.co.za
Website: www.djuma.com
Reservations Tel: +27 (0)13 735 5118

BOTANICAL INDEX

Brown Ivory – *Berchemia discolor*
Common Wild Fig – *Ficus thonningii*
Fever Tree – *Acacia xanthophloea*
Jackalberry – *Diospyros mespilifor*
Knobthorn – *Acacia nigrescens*
Marula – *Sclerocarya birrea*
Red Bush Willow – *Combretum apiculatum*
Strangler Fig – *Ficus craterostoma*
Tree Wisteria – *Bolusanthus speciosus*
Weeping Boer-bean – *Schotia brachypetala*
Wild Olive – *Olea europaea* (subspecies) *africana*